The Website Workout

The Website Workout

A simple, complete guide to strengthening your online presence

Darin Brockman

Viva Books

New Delhi | Mumbai | Chennai | Kolkata | Bangalore | Hyderabad | Kochi | Guwahati

First Indian Edition 2010

VIVA BOOKS PRIVATE LIMITED

- 4737/23, Ansari Road, Daryaganj, New Delhi 110 002
  E-mail: vivadelhi@vivagroupindia.net, Tel. 42242200
- Plot No. 76, Service Industries, Shirvane, Sector 1, Nerul, Navi Mumbai 400 706
  E-mail: vivamumbai@vivagroupindia.net, Tel. 27721273, 27721274
- Jamals Fazal Chambers, 26 Greams Road, Chennai 600 006
  E-mail: vivachennai@vivagroupindia.net, Tel. 28290304, 28294241
- B-103, Jindal Towers, 21/1A/3 Darga Road, Kolkata 700 017
  E-mail: vivakolkata@vivagroupindia.net, Tel. 22836381, 22816713
- 7, Sovereign Park Apartments, 56-58, K. R. Road, Basavanagudi, Bangalore 560 004
  E-mail: vivabangalore@vivagroupindia.net, Tel. 26607409, 26607410
- 101-102 Mughal Marc Apartments, 3-4-637 to 641, Narayanguda, Hyderabad 500 029
  E-mail: vivahyderabad@vivagroupindia.net, Tel. 27564481, 27564482
- Beevi Towers, First Floor, SRM Road, Kaloor, Kochi 682018, Kerala
  E-mail: vivakochi@vivagroupindia.net, Tel. 0484-2403055, 2403056
- 232, GNB Road, Beside UCO Bank, Silpukhuri, Guwahati 781 003
  E-mail: vivaguwahati@vivagroupindia.net, Tel. 0361-2666386

Published by arrangement with
Words at Work, London
West Hill House
6 Swains Lane
London N6 6QS
United Kingdom

ISBN: 978-81-309-1311-7

Published by Vinod Vasishtha for Viva Books Private Limited, 4737/23 Ansari Road, Daryaganj, New Delhi 110 002. Printed and bound by Raj Press, R-3, Inderpuri, New Delhi 110 012.

CONTENTS

Preface vi

Introduction vii

1 **Objectives** 1

2 **Research** 13

3 **Presentation** 25

4 **Content** 47

5 **Architecture** 61

6 **Optimisation** 83

7 **E-commerce** 95

8 **E-marketing** 111

9 **Management** 127

10 **Analytics** 141

Appendices

Acronyms and abbreviations 155

Glossary of terms 157

Selected references and useful websites 167

Index 171

PREFACE

A DECADE AGO I talked about websites as brochures for businesses. Now I talk about business through websites, for they have become an integral part of any successful business.

I have many people to thank for helping me on the long road of putting together the material for this book. Had I known the process was more of a marathon than a sprint I might have shied away from it, but I am very proud of the end result and, from my many years of working in the website development field, I know it will fill a great gap in the market.

My sincerest thanks go to Kay Sayce for her wisdom, knowledge and patience in extracting from me the mass of information in my head on the subject, giving it shape and coherence, and making it accessible to business leaders who need a useful, engaging and clearly written guide to strengthening their online presence.

I would like to thank the whole team at BCL NuMedia not only for their help during the development of the book and taking on work process changes that I introduced because of new knowledge derived from my research for it, but also for their work and support for the company over the years. Jamie Crawford, Drew Laignel, Dennis Panchenko, Andi Rivers, Mark Tucker, Carol Bartlam and Lynda Morten – my thanks to them all for working with me and sharing their knowledge. And special thanks to Martin Reed for taking on the task of creating much of the artwork for the book and for always exceeding my expectations.

I'd also like to thank Natasha for her support, and my mother Rosalyn for always being there and guiding my personal growth and my businesses. And thanks also to my clients for giving me the reason and the knowledge to produce this book.

Darin Brockman

INTRODUCTION

THE INTERNET HAS COME OF AGE and the virtual shop is here. You are in business and you have something to sell – products, services, or both. These days you are expected to do this, at least in part, online. But you're not sure what this involves. What do you need to know?

Welcome to *The Website Workout*. Its purpose is to tell you what you need to know. Pursuing the fitness analogy, think of this book as your personal trainer, here to guide you through information, insights and exercises – gentle at first, and then gradually becoming a little more strenuous – that will leave you better equipped to make decisions about how to strengthen your online presence.

The book assumes that you are in business, that you are not necessarily familiar with website technology and jargon, and that you know that if you're going to achieve your business objectives you need a top quality website. It follows a logical step-by-step process, using simple, everyday language to guide you through unfamiliar territory by encouraging you to ask and answer a set of questions:

- What do you want your website to do? (*Objectives*)
- Who are your competitors and customers? (*Research*)
- What should your website look like? (*Presentation*)
- What information should it carry? (*Content*)
- What functions should it have? (*Architecture*)
- How do you get it high on the search engine listings? (*Optimisation*)
- How do you maximise your online trading? (*E-commerce*)
- How do you maximise your online marketing? (*E-marketing*)
- What tools and strategies do you need to maintain the website? (*Management*)
- How do you assess its performance and what changes might be needed? (*Analytics*)

Each of these questions forms the basis of a chapter in this book. Before you start thinking about building or revamping your website in order to increase your revenue and broaden your customer base, do read the book from cover to cover.

The net is here to stay and it is changing the way business is done. Reading, absorbing and applying the information and insights in *The Website Workout* will help you to participate, successfully, in that change.

Chapter 1

OBJECTIVES

YOU HAVE SET UP a new business and you want to create a website through which you can successfully market and sell your products.* Or you already have a business website but, for various reasons, you want to revamp it. Or you want to build microsites linked to your existing website.

This book discusses the elements – visual, textual and technical – that go into building and managing a successful website.

Accompanying the text are guidelines, examples and diagrams aimed at making it easy for you to understand the detail of what is, for many people, a complex subject.

But before you get into that detail, there are four simple, but crucial, questions you need to ask yourself:

- Why do I want a new website?
- What do I want my website to do?
- What is my customer base?
- What is my competition?

Unless you're clear about the answers to these questions, your website will probably miss its mark, and you will have spent time and money on something that is not going to do what you want it to do. If you can provide clear answers to these questions, however, you will have gone some way towards laying the foundations for a successful website.

In this chapter, I deal with the answers to the first two questions. In Chapter 2, I talk about the research you need to do on your customer base and your competitors.

** Throughout this book the term 'products' is used to cover both products and services.*

Why do you want a new website?

When I ask new clients this question, I get a variety of answers. In some cases, they've clearly thought about it. Sometimes they seem a bit thrown. And occasionally there are conflicting answers, one person giving a set of reasons quite different from those that someone else puts forward (see Box 1.1, page 4).

Here are some typical answers to the question:

- we want to create brand awareness / raise our profile / improve our image
- we want to add an additional revenue stream to our business
- more people are buying online now, so we want to start selling online
- we want to make the net a core element of our marketing strategy
- we think a good website might reduce our marketing costs
- we'd like a website that attracts as many sales enquiries as... (*name of competitor*)
- our current website is a bit static, like a brochure – it needs to be updated and more lively
- we want more interaction with our customers, to understand their needs better

At this point in a meeting I usually say something along the lines of: "Let's dig a little deeper, and then we'll come back, later, to the issue of what exactly you want your website to do."

It is also at this point, by the way, that I remind clients setting up a new business to register the domain name and set up the corresponding e-mail address. Getting the domain name right is important, so do take time over this.

BOX 1.1 Conflicting objectives

It's common for the people responsible for commissioning a new website to have conflicting ideas about the purpose of the site. Here is a typical scenario.

A garden furniture business decided to get quotes from web development agencies to build a new website. Their old one was a bit rusty and they wanted a new look and a lot more functionality. The two directors asked for a meeting with my agency. Things were going well until I asked: "The revenue streams you envisage for your site – where do you see them coming from, in the short and the long term?"

They hadn't talked to each about that. One had a clear idea about possible future revenue streams, but the other didn't seem to have thought about it at all and began to disagree with his colleague's ideas. I had to sit back until they agreed on where the company was going, so that we had an idea of the site scalability needed to cater for future plans.

What is your business and where is it going?

What type of business do you have? What are your main revenue streams? Do you advertise? What are your business processes? Do you use wholesalers? Do you occupy a specific niche? What are your short-term plans? Do you plan to add new revenue streams? Where do you want the business to go in the long term?

These are just some of the questions I might ask new clients about their businesses. I need to know the answers to them for two reasons:

- to categorise the business in website terms
- to cater for changes and the future development of the website

Categories

Broadly, most websites fall into one of the categories in Figure 1.1 (page 6). There is, inevitably, some overlap between the categories (e.g., e-commerce websites might have an entertainment element;

online magazine websites might carry e-commerce facilities; and online free service websites might feature forums). Nevertheless, you should be able to allocate your business to one or more of the seven categories.

Why is this important? Each category is characterised by particular tried-and-tested features, so unless you know what category your business falls into, you might not know enough about what features would suit your website. Another reason is that when your website has been built you'll need to know which directory categories to submit it to, as part of the process of optimising it (see Chapter 6); this will be easy if your own categorisation is clear.

Whatever category your website falls into, you need to be clear about one overriding fact: all websites in all categories share a common goal – to generate income. Some websites make money directly (e.g., from online sales of products or from donations to a cause). Others make it indirectly (e.g., by raising a company's profile or by carrying advertisements). Either way, all websites are set up to increase revenue.

BOX 1.2 A money-making website?

A group of people built what they called a 'corporate alumni' site. The people in the group were former employees of a top international company, and they decided to build a site that would enable all past and current company employees (about 30,000 people) to network with each other, paying a small subscription to register on the site and to use it to exchange information on jobs, events, 'where are we now', etc.

On the face of it, apart from recouping the cost of building the site by charging a subscription, it's not immediately clear where the profit in this site comes from. But the group were convinced that, if done well enough, the site would be popular and the company might want to buy it (as a useful resource for recruitment, mailing lists, staff relations, etc.). And indeed that's what happened. The site was popular and the company bought it for a significant sum.

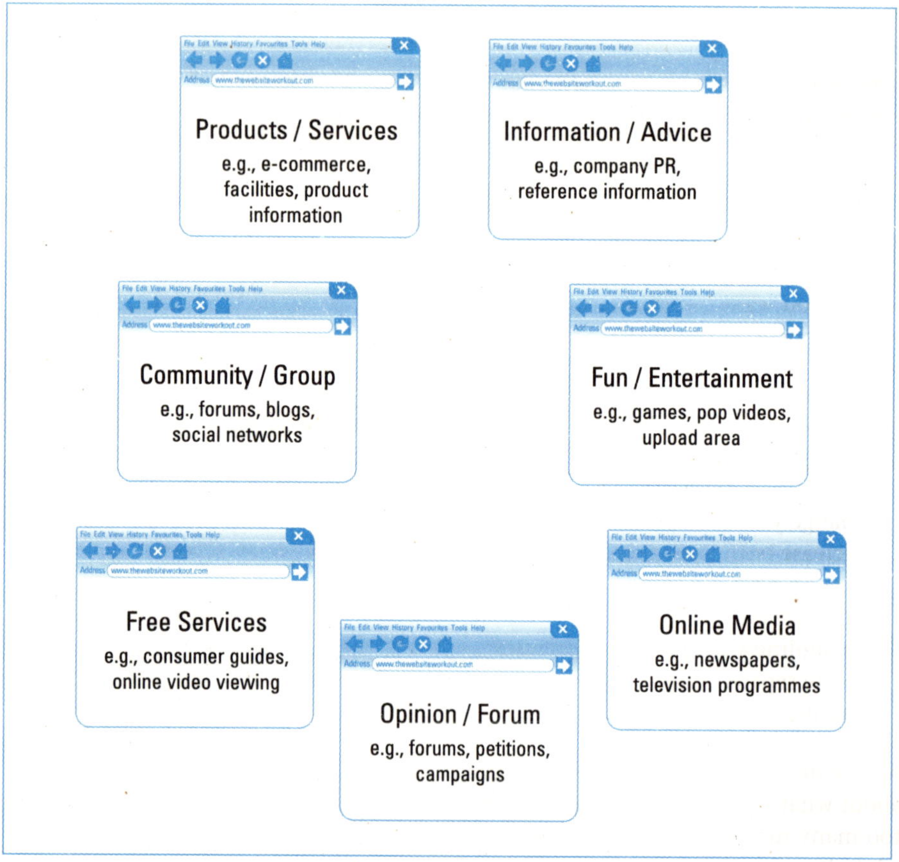

FIGURE 1.1 The main categories of websites

It's important to be clear about which category your website falls into. In which category would you put these well-known sites? amazon.co.uk; bbc.co.uk; bebo.com; bloomberg.com; facebook.com; ft.com; gocompare.com; google.com; play.com; sourceforge.net; stopwar.co.uk; supershareware.com; virgin.com; wikipedia.org; williamhillpoker.com

Future development

What do you want your business to achieve? What are your long-term plans for it? Do you want to sell your products to more countries? Do you want to offer new services that complement those you currently offer? Do you want to create new revenue streams linked to your present products?

You need to think in detail about where you want your business to be a few years ahead and how you intend to get there. For example, within 5 years you want to expand your customer base by 30% and double your turnover, primarily by expanding your product range. How will you lay the foundations for this within the site you want to build now?

Or you might, in a few years time, want to do one or more of the following:

- change your sales emphasis from offline to online
- increase both the range and type of products you offer
- take on a whole new product range through a merger
- integrate elements of your warehousing procedures into your website
- streamline your business processes
- create separate community areas when you expand into foreign countries / languages

A note of caution here. It's very tempting at this point to go overboard about what you want to achieve and to weigh down your website with too many functions. A website can do all sorts of extraordinary things when it comes to streamlining and developing your business, but don't make it more complicated or ambitious than it needs to be.

Be clear not just about what you want your website to do, but also about what it *cannot* do, *doesn't need* to do or *shouldn't* do.

Ideally, having thought about all the things you want your business to achieve, you should now create a shortlist of core objectives (say, four

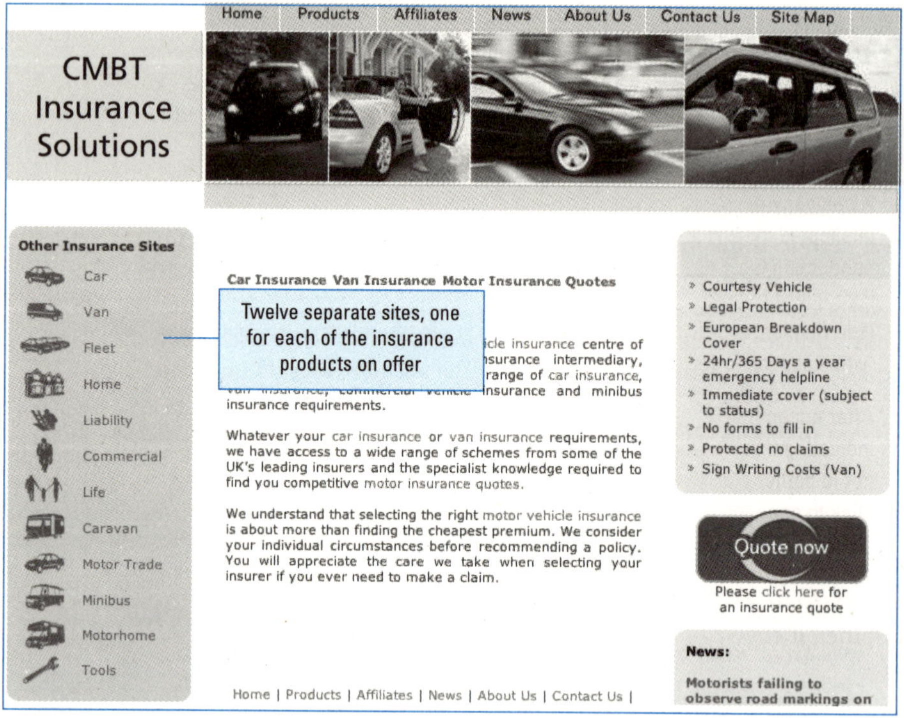

FIGURE 1.2 Planning for the future

An insurance firm wanted to set up sites for each of its main insurance products – 12 in all. This meant revamping their current site and building 12 new ones incorporating the branding of the main site and being paid for as revenue came in from the sites already built.

Sales took off, exceeding expectations, and the firm decided to run a national TV advertising campaign. But asking viewers to go to one of 12 sites, depending on the product they wanted, would not work, so a new site was built, consolidating all 12 products in one place. Had the initial budget and time constraints not been there, it would have been more cost-effective to have built just one large site in the first place. And it would have pleased the search engines!

BOX 1.3 Overdoing it

It's tempting with a new website to load it up with functions that you don't really need, costing you more than you need to pay.

A company asked us to quote for building a website in English that could then be duplicated in four other languages – quite an expensive process. We suggested conducting four AdWord campaigns first, one in each of the foreign languages, to see if people in the countries being targeted would click through to the Google Ads (see Chapter 8). The company agreed and we set up four AdWord campaigns, each with a limit of £300.

After a month of monitoring them, in not one case had the money been used up, indicating that there would be very little traffic on these sites. It was then easy to decide not to bother with the expense of creating the foreign language sites, but to stick to one language, English.

to six). Go over this shortlist carefully to ensure that, one way or another, it covers everything. And then prioritise the items on the list.

How can your website help you achieve your objectives?

Once a new client has told me why he wants a new website, and we've talked about his business and what he wants it to achieve, we then discuss the possible ways in which a website could help him do this.* And he now begins to see why it's so important to be clear about his business and its future, and why ill-defined or poorly conceived objectives could lead to website problems, frustrated ambitions and wasted expenditure.

---

* *Throughout this book we use 'he' and 'his' in a generic sense, rather than the more cumbersome 'he / she' or 'his / hers'.*

If your website is to help you achieve your objectives it must, in the first instance, attract visitors. There are many ways to do this, all of which we discuss in more detail in later chapters. They include:

- optimising the site architecture
- optimising the site content
- building incoming links to the site
- web-based marketing (affiliate marketing, blogs, newsfeeds, etc.)
- pay-per-click (PPC) campaigns
- e-mail marketing campaigns

Attracting visitors to your website is one thing. Keeping them there is quite another. Visitors usually take just a few seconds to decide whether or not to stay on a website. They want to see, quickly, if what you offer is what they're looking for. But if it takes them more than a few seconds to see this, they move on. And you've probably lost them.

The secret in tempting visitors to stay is to present them with a clear, simple site – clear in its message and simple in its navigation. Going back to my earlier suggestion that you create a shortlist of prioritised core objectives, one of the reasons for this was that if these objectives

BOX 1.4 Discovering new markets

For many years, one of our clients, a manufacturer of industrial products, had a website that was little more than a brochure and targeted four sectors – aerospace, building and construction, electrics and electronics, and general engineering. They decided that it was time to get into e-commerce and asked us to build an e-commerce site for them.

A year later, not only had the site increased the company's revenue, it had also identified seven new market sectors they had never explored – arts and crafts, casting and tooling, defence, education and research, filtration, marine industry, and traffic management. So a bigger and better site was built to cater for all the additional sectors, with the increase in revenue over the preceding year paying for the cost of developing the new site.

BOX 1.5 Reflecting your objectives on your website

Some clients work hard on prioritising their core objectives, but then fail to reflect those priorities in the material they supply to a web development agency to build the site.

One of our clients had stressed customer relations, including liaison with sales agents and distributors, as a top priority for their website. But their PowerPoint presentation showing their vision for the site didn't reflect this. We had to completely revise the way they had categorised the content, to give greater prominence to the site's customer relations features (e.g., logins, trade area, contact information, feedback opportunities).

By contrast, a training institution told us that it had three priority objectives for its new site: to provide information on courses, to publicise a new service (consultancy) and to equip the site with useful resources (e.g., newsfeeds, glossary). The content they sent us for the site reflected these priorities. We didn't have to revise it or ask for more. They were clear about what they wanted, which made it easy for us to deliver what they wanted.

are clear, then your site stands a much greater chance of being clear and simple, and thus tempting your visitors to stay. A great example of clarity and simplicity is Google's home page – a white page with just a logo and a search box. No fuss, no bother, no flashing lights.

Now you need to encourage your visitors to explore your website and, ultimately, to buy your product, if not today, then tomorrow. So your website needs to be a comfortable, up-to-date and interesting place to stay, with easy navigation, comprehensive information, useful resources and good opportunities for interaction (e.g., forums, videos, glossary, product sheets, online catalogue, contact information).

And what about the behind-the-scenes aspect of the website? What can it do that will simplify and streamline your business processes? How can it help with, for example, stocktaking, distributor liaison, document management, processing orders, invoicing and delivery, in order to cut down on the time and costs that these processes incur in the offline world? These are all issues you need to think about when looking at how your website can help you achieve your objectives.

What do you want your website to do?

You should now be able to answer the all-important question: What do you want your website to do? You are clear about why you want a new website, what category your website would fall into, and what the main revenue streams are likely to be in both the short term and the long term. You've taken note of the things that can go wrong along the way and cost you time and money, such as building a site that fails to cater for future plans or being too ambitious about what you want the site to achieve. With all this done, you are almost ready to conduct the research needed to learn more about your customers and your competitors.

There is one last item to take into account, though. Your budget. How much do you want to spend on building and running the website? How much can you afford? The important issue here is to remember that the cost of building a site is not the whole cost. Once a site has been launched, there are the running costs, and you need to factor these into your overall budget. It's generally safe to budget on the basis that:

- 60% of your budget will go on the one-off costs of building the site (e.g., presentation, architecture, content development, e-commerce features, database development, and search engine optimisation)
- 40% of your budget will go on the running costs (e.g., monthly hosting fee, content management licence, optimisation, e-marketing campaigns, analytics reports, and support package fees)

So, keep your objectives within the parameters of what, realistically, you can afford to spend on building and running a successful website.

Chapter 2

RESEARCH

YOU HAVE LOOKED AT how a new website can help you achieve your business objectives, so you now have a clearer idea of what you want this website to do. But there is now some research to do before work on building the site can begin. This research relates to two main areas:

- your customers
- your competitors

When I meet new clients I assume that, whether they're a start-up or have been in business for some time, they have a fair idea of who – in the offline world – their main customers and competitors are. If they didn't, they wouldn't have a viable business.

They will, or should, know what market segment their business is aimed at, what characterises this segment in terms of needs, interests and opportunities, and how to reach this segment offline. And they will, or should, know who their main offline competitors are, their competitors' profiles in terms of size, geographical coverage, niche, product range and marketing strategy, and what their market position is in relation to their competitors.

What they are less likely to know is who their main customers and competitors are in *the online world*. While the principles underlying customer and competitor analyses in the offline and online worlds are similar, there are significant differences in how to conduct these analyses.

Whether you're a start-up or an existing business operating in both the offline and online worlds, or a new business operating only online, this

---

We use the terms 'customers' and 'visitors' for the people looking at websites, the former when the context is clearly related to buying products and services, and the latter when the meaning is broader.

chapter provides guidelines on how to research your online customer base and your competitors, and what implications your research findings have for your website.

Your customers

Some businesses link directly to their end-users. Others reach them indirectly via wholesalers, distributors, affiliated companies and / or other 'middlemen'. And, in many cases, businesses combine the direct and indirect approaches.

Thus, there are two customer bases your website might be aimed at:

- the people who use your products (your end-users)
- the people through whom you market your products (your 'middlemen')

Let's deal with the end-users first. You need to establish, right at the outset, whether or not there is an online market. This is crucial. Every week I get calls from people who say they've come up with a great idea for a website and that it's bound to make them millions because no one else seems to have thought of it. I'll usually say something like: "There's probably a very good reason why no one else seems to be doing it – because there *is* no online market and therefore no revenue!"

Or they have come up with a great idea, but haven't done any research. If they had, they would have found that the market place is well served already, there's no room for more. People will often spend thousands of pounds on creating an online business in an overcrowded market place. But when someone tells me they have a great idea and it does indeed sound like one, I suggest they do some more research before coming back to me.

BOX 2.1 Researching a website idea

In 2005 two brothers came into our office with what they said was a great idea for a website. They wanted to know what it would cost to build. The idea centred around online personalised 'talking cards' – visitors go onto the site, record a message, choose a card, and send it out. The idea looked good, but they hadn't done any research, online or offline, so I suggested they did some and then come back to us.

They researched the web, but found no sites selling what they proposed selling. They visited dozens of greetings cards shops, including all the major UK chains, and asked about 'talking card' sales. They contacted some local companies, to see if there'd be a market in the corporate world (e.g., company Christmas cards).

Everything pointed towards the idea being viable, so they came back to us with market information and their idea now finely honed, and we set about building the site. It wasn't cheap, but the success of the venture meant they soon recovered the site development costs.

There are several things you can do to find out if there is an online market and, if it does exist, what exactly it wants:

- conduct a survey among your current offline customer base, if you have one (e.g., ask them if they buy products online; if they do, which types of products; would they buy *your* products online; what online information would they need before making a purchase; what delivery times would they expect); although these customers are 'offline' in that they buy your products offline, most of them will have e-mail addresses, so conduct the survey via e-mail

- conduct an e-mail survey among your current online customer base, if you have one but want to expand it or reach a new market, or both (see Figure 2.1)

- compile a list of keywords that describe your product (say, 10 phrases) and run it through Google AdWords (see Chapter 8) to find out how much the keywords cost and the click-through needed for there to be a good return on investment; this exercise will also give you an idea of the product's popularity among online customers (in the website world, the term 'keywords' is used to denote both single words and phrases)

1. How do you rate our current site? Very Good / Good / OK / Poor / Very Poor

2. What further information would you like on the site?

3. Did you find the contact/product information easy to find? Yes / No

4. How often do you buy online? Daily / Weekly / Monthly / Rarely / Never

5. In addition to our usual product range, we shall soon be selling (*name of product*) online. Would you buy (*name of product*)? Yes / No

FIGURE 2.1 A sample page from an online customer survey questionnaire

Note the use of multiple choice questions. Survey respondents usually prefer questions in this format because they don't take up too much time. Sites that will help you prepare and conduct an online survey include www.questionpro.com, www.checkbox.com, www.zapsurvey.com and www.vote-pro.com

- study your online competitors' customer base (e.g., look at their websites to see who their target groups are; how they're selling their products; how big their market place is; where to place your products in that market place; what new opportunities that market place might offer)

- look at some of the many miscellaneous online sources of information that might give you some insight into your potential customer base (e.g., blogs, newsfeeds, e-newsletters, social network sites and customer surveys related to your market sector)

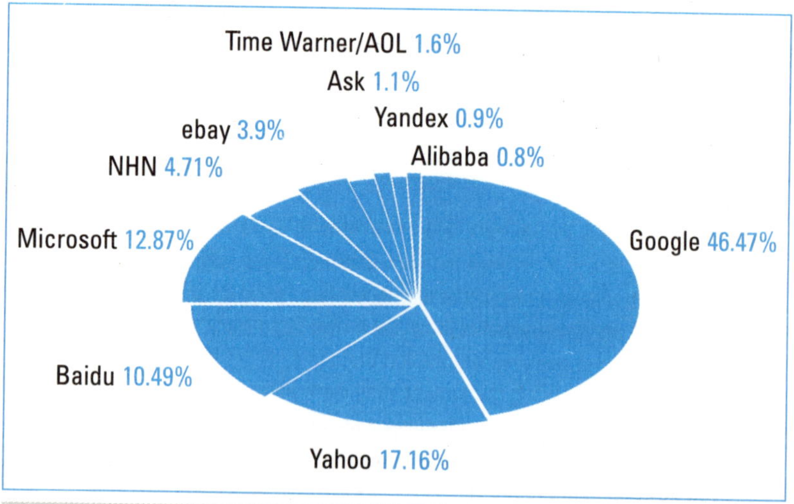

FIGURE 2.2 The major search engines (% market share worldwide, 2007)

When you are conducting research on your current and potential customers and competitors, remember that there are more than one or two search engines to consult. It's worth looking at the top four at least and, in the long term, being aware of the others in case their market share grows substantially.

Source: http://en.wikipedia.org/wiki/searchengines

When you've done all this, you'll not only have found out more about your current and potential customers and their needs, but probably also have found online customer bases that you didn't even know existed.

Dealing with the second group – the middlemen – is more straightforward. You already know who makes up this customer base. What you need to know is what they want your website to do. Send them a questionnaire seeking the information you want (e.g., ask them how they use your current website, if you have one; do they find the site useful; is it easy to find the information they need on the site; could the technical, product and processing information on the site be improved; what other information would they like to see on the site; was the contact information easy to find).

BOX 2.2 Addressing the needs of your distributors

After a survey of his distributors, one of our clients saw that it would be useful if his website had a secure login area for each distributor, carrying all product information and documentation relating only to that distributor (e.g., product specifications, delivery times, cost estimates and forecasted cost savings). The login areas were set up, each retaining the client brand and carrying information that the distributors could access at the press of a button, thus enhancing the service they were able to give during meetings with potential customers and giving our client a competitive edge.

Your competitors

Conducting an analysis of your online competitors will take you into territory that might be unfamiliar. You will come across, for example, software analytical tools you might not have heard of, website functions you didn't know existed and online marketing strategies you have only the vaguest notion about.

Although it might be a bit difficult to grasp everything at this stage, once you've read the whole book it will all fall into place and you shouldn't have any problem understanding how to analyse your online competitors. For example, in this chapter I touch on search engine optimisation (SEO) – not an easy subject – but after you've read the rest of the book (particularly Chapter 6) you'll know all about SEO.

What do you need to know about your online competitors? The first thing is who the main ones are. Here are some steps for finding this out:

- type in some keywords relating to your business, and see what sites they bring up (use more than one search engine if possible)

- go to as many of these sites as time allows, look at their priority pages (e.g., home page, product pages) and see what the keywords on these page are; this involves going to their site, clicking on 'View' and then on 'Page Source'; this brings up a page of code, in which there should be the title 'Keywords' followed by a list of those used for the site (see Figure 2.3, colour page I)

- narrow down the number of sites by typing in what you now think are the most appropriate keywords, and then narrow this number down still further by being even more specific

- now look at the first page of search engine results pages (SERPS) and make a note of sites at or near the top that:
  - have paid to be there (the 'sponsored links' sites at the top of the page, usually on a light-coloured background; and the narrow right-hand 'sponsored links' column)
  - have *not* paid to be there (the sites in the so-called 'organic' or 'natural' listings that appear below or next to the sponsored sites)

Although you need to be aware of the sponsored sites, the important sites are those at or near the top of the organic listings. They are there because of their content. 'Content' means 'the information on a site and how this information is conveyed' (see Chapter 4). Their content and other SEO factors have given them the edge, from an online marketing point of view. So those companies at or near the top of the organic listings are your true online competitors.

Having identified your main competitors, you now need to find out more about them. This involves analysing their site content. As this is quite a lot of work, out of your top 10 online competitors choose, say, only three or four – the ones you're most likely to be competing with – and follow these steps:

- go to the search engine search box and type in 'links:' followed by a space and the competitor's URL (e.g., links: www.bcl-numedia.com); this will bring up the number of links into the site (see Figure 2.4, page 22); the more incoming links a site has, the more successful it is likely to be; this will give you an idea of how many links you need to build

- go to the competitor site itself and, via 'View' in the top menu, open 'Page Source'; this will bring up its keywords, as described earlier; use them to obtain a keyword ranking analysis (see Chapter 6), showing how your current site ranks against this competitor site (software that will do this for you includes Web Position Gold and Web CEO)

- on the competitor site, check its traffic by using web information software (e.g., Alexa) to tell you how much traffic it gets, where the traffic comes from and what site pages tend to be the most popular

- visit some of the resources on the competitor site, such as chat rooms, newsletters, community areas and newsfeeds, and see how they work, if they seem to be popular, which ones might be worth having on your site, and what resources you could provide that your competitor doesn't

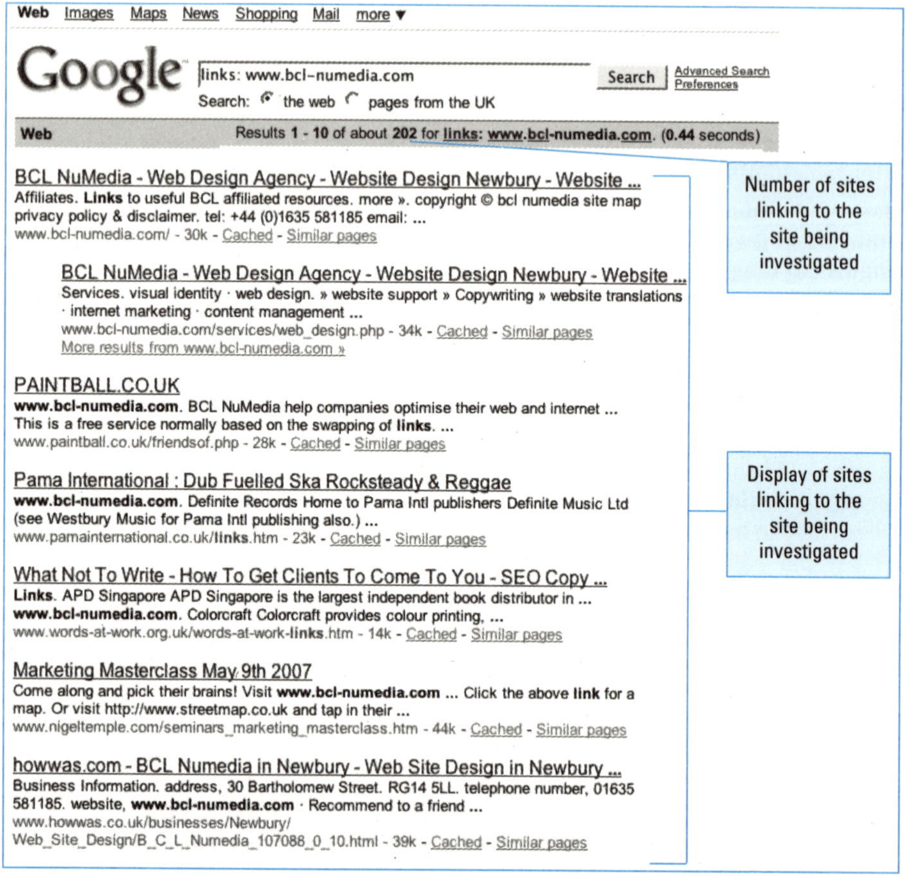

FIGURE 2.4 Checking competitors' incoming links

Entering 'links' in the search box, followed by a space, followed by the URL of the competitor site that you want to investigate will show you how many incoming links that site has and where they are coming from. Note that the search engine listings will also always include entries for the competitor site itself.

All these activities relate to analysing site content. Do you also need to take account of what a site looks like (its 'presentation', see Chapter 3)? The answer is, only as a secondary consideration. You may find that some competitors' sites lack a professional appearance, and yet they're among the top entries in the organic listings. Some very basic-looking sites rank high because they are heavy on content and incoming links (e.g., more than 1000 indexed pages and at least 500 incoming links) and are not stuffed with Flash or too many images, allowing search engines to index them easily (see Figure 2.5). So focus most attention on your competitors' site content.

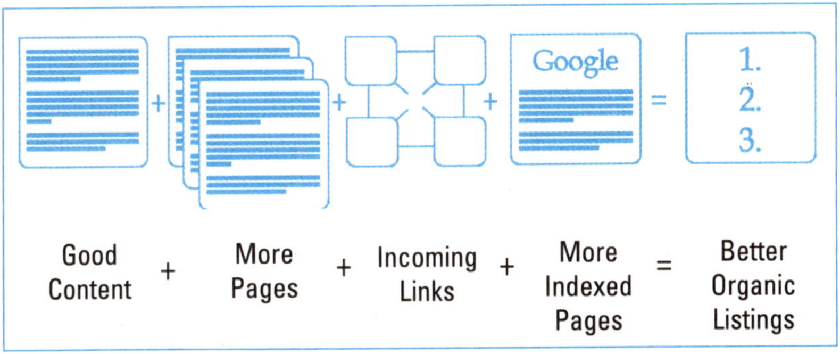

FIGURE 2.5 Good content results in higher listings

Checking competitors' sites involves looking at site content, including the number of indexed pages and incoming links that these sites have. This information will give you an idea of what your site should try to achieve.

How has your research helped?

By the end of the first chapter, I had established a list of possible features and functions you need to consider incorporating into your website if you are to achieve your current and future business objectives. In this chapter, I dug a little deeper, showing you how to analyse your current and potential online customers and competitors.

These analyses will have taught you something about websites in general, what they comprise and what makes them work. They will also have given you hands-on experience at exploring websites and their content, making it easier for you to understand the more technical aspects discussed in much of the rest of this book. More specifically, the analyses will have given you the insight into *your* customers and competitors that you need to incorporate into your site.

For your online customers, you should now be able to answer these questions:

- Who are my online customers?
- What are their needs and interests?
- What would they expect to find on my website?
- How can my website cater for their needs, interests and expectations?

For your online competitors, you should now be able to answer these questions:

- Who are my main online competitors?
- How does my business resemble theirs and how does it differ?
- What content and resource factors account for their success?
- Should I apply these factors to my website and, if so, how?
- How can I make my website more attractive for visitors?

And now, armed with your answers to these questions and a clearer understanding of what you want your website to do, work can start on creating the site and on achieving the ultimate goal of increasing your revenue.

Chapter 3

PRESENTATION

YOU HAVE ANALYSED and answered these questions: Why do I want a new website? What do I want it to do? Who are my online customers? Who are my main online competitors? You should now be clear about what your website can and should do, and the work can start on creating it.

There are three main components of a website:

- *presentation:* the visual component (e.g., size, layout, typography, colour, images)
- *content:* the textual component (e.g., text, keywords, tags, downloads)
- *architecture:* the technical component (e.g., structure, functions, databases)

The three components of a website do overlap, of course, but to understand and apply the principles of each one you need to look at them separately. In this chapter the focus is on presentation, and in Chapters 4 and 5 it is on content and architecture. Thus, by the start of Chapter 6, I will have laid the visual, textual and technical foundations of a website that should generate new revenue streams for you.

The evolution of websites

In the early 1990s websites were little more than a set of electronic documents that were compiled and managed by 'webmasters' and resided in IT departments. They were created to provide information.

With the increasing specialisation in website development, there is a growing tendency to draw a clear line between 'web design' and 'web development'. In this book we use 'design' and 'designer' only in relation to presentation, whereas 'web development' is used when referring to building the whole site, and 'developer' when referring to an agency or person who builds websites.

BOX 3.1 Choosing a web development agency

Once you have listed and prioritised your objectives and done some research on your customers and competitors, it's time to decide how you are going get the site built. Buy a web development application (e.g., DreamWeaver CS3) and have a go at doing it yourself? Or get a web development agency to build the structure and the databases? Handle the presentation and content in-house? Or outsource them to a graphic design agency and a copywriter?

A golden rule in business is 'stick to what you're good at'. If your company has experienced programmers who know what goes into creating a successful e-commerce site and what software to use, then by all means build your site in-house. If not, leave it to the experts. Don't be tempted to think that building the site in-house will give you greater control over the site once it is built. A good development agency, when it has built your site, will give you all the tools, support and instruction you need to manage your site when it goes live.

What they looked like didn't matter and how they operated wasn't based on any rules. Then, in 1994, a group of people (including Tim Berners-Lee, who had invented the World Wide Web in 1989) established the World Wide Web Consortium (W3C) to develop universal web standards and guidelines. The Consortium's overall goal was 'web inter-operability' – consensus on web protocols and compatibility of web technologies.

As more and more people began using the web, marketing departments started to see websites as marketing tools and wanted to incorporate graphics into them. But HTML, the language of the web, was never intended to support graphics (see Chapter 5), so the developers of the major browsers at the time (see Figure 3.1, page 28) had to start adding extensions to HTML to enable it to do so. Over time, what was originally designed as a simple language for displaying documents was tweaked and extended to such a degree, with each browser adopting a

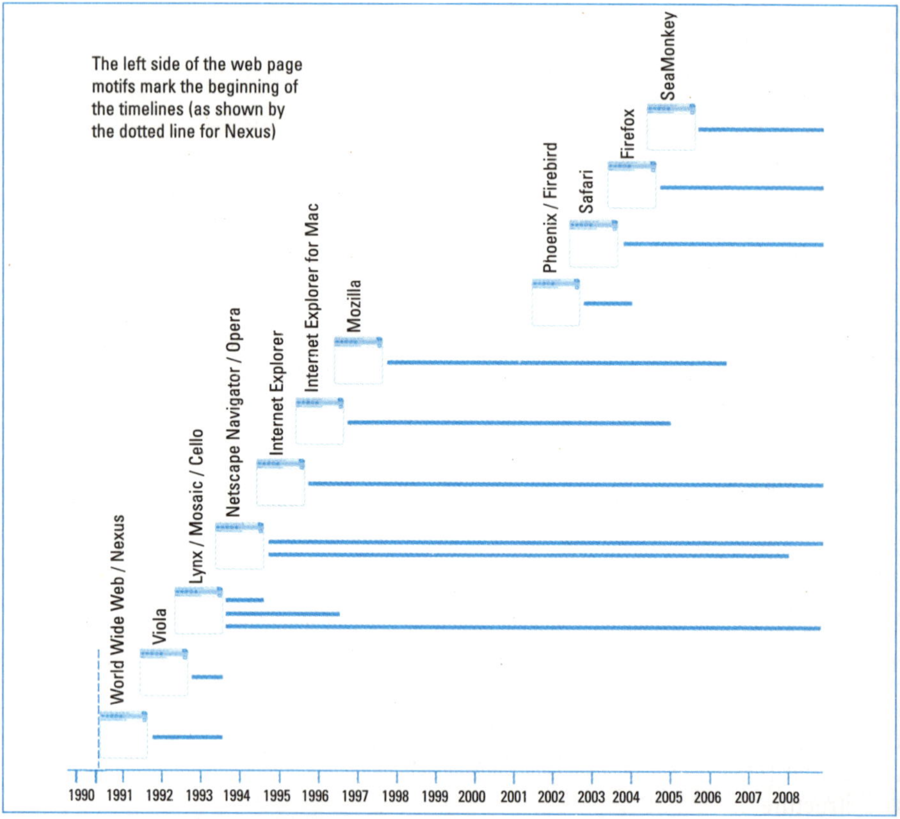

FIGURE 3.1 Web browser timeline

The first browser (Nexus) appeared in 1990. Then more browsers (e.g., Netscape, Internet Explorer) appeared, varying greatly in the colours, typefaces and images they could 'see' on a site, which meant developers had to write different codes for different browsers. In 1998, to stop the so-called 'browser wars', W3C launched the Web Standards Project (WSP) to bring browser companies into line. In 2002, W3C re-launched the WSP, this time aiming it at web developers. Compatible browsers (e.g., Firefox, Safari) began to appear, heralding a new dawn for website access.

different approach to the problem, that it all became a rather complicated mess. Elements of HTML designed for displaying data in tables ('table-based') were used to control layout, and simple changes to layout or to other presentation factors such as colours or typefaces could take hours, and even then still not be rendered correctly on some platforms.

At about this time, in the mid-1990s, a programming language called Javascript arrived and enabled everyone to liven up their sites a bit with such features as drop-down menus and mouseover effects – and everyone did. But it was a client-side rather than a server-side facility (see Chapter 5) and was often more of a hindrance than a help. A server-side programming language called Perl was being used by some website developers for more advanced functionality, such as handling contact forms, but its complexity limited its popularity.

All this resulted in the rather clumsy, brochure-like sites of the late 1990s. Website-building software (e.g., Dreamweaver and Front Page) came on stream, leading to a proliferation of dull, static sites.

A breakthrough came when the Cascading Style Sheets (CSS) language began to be widely adopted in about 2002. CSS was created to handle the presentation aspects of a website, separately from HTML, which meant that HTML could revert to being used, as intended, for content and structure. In fact, its successor, XHTML, does not allow you to use it for presentation – this all has to be done using CSS.

Out went the frustrations of trying to make HTML do things it wasn't meant to do; now the different components of a site could be worked on separately, with the right tools, and integrated when appropriate. Out went table-based sites; now sites could be built on more flexible, free-flowing foundations. And out went superfluous graphics and the excessive use of Javascript; now, sites looked cleaner and more professional.

But it was not until the arrival of scripting languages written specifically for the web, as well as affordable database software and better browsers (e.g., Firefox, Opera and Safari, all more W3C compliant than the browsers of the 1990s), that websites began to move on from the static, template-based sites generated by Dreamweaver and Front Page. Developers took advantage of the many new technologies, such as PHP / MySQL and ASP / SQL (see Chapter 5), that enabled them to create dynamic content with which visitors could interact, such as bulletin boards, messaging and social networking. Website development had come of age (see Figure 3.2, colour page II).

Why is presentation important?

It takes no more than half a minute for a visitor landing on a page on your website to form an impression of your business. What boxes is he ticking in those first seconds? Probably these ones (and probably subconsciously):

- Did I get to this page with no problems?
- Is it what I was expecting?
- Does it look professional?
- Does it look interesting and inviting?
- Is it attractive, clean and uncluttered?
- Does it look easy to explore?
- Shall I stay and explore it?

If all the answers are 'yes', your website presentation has passed the test set by your sternest critic – and the only critic that really matters – your target customer.

So, the most important question to ask when creating your website presentation is: Who is the site being designed for? The answer should be: My customers. Many businesses overlook this, focusing instead on a presentation that they think will impress other designers and other businesses. But it doesn't necessarily impress their target customers. So the half-minute ticks by, few or none of the boxes are ticked, and a potential customer moves on and is lost, probably, to a competitor.

The next question is: Who should design the presentation? Because the first impression your site creates is crucial to encouraging visitors to stay, explore and ultimately buy, you cannot afford to cut costs on the presentation. Website presentation is a specialist skill and, to get it right, you need a specialist to do it.

A word of caution here. Ensure that the specialist is more than just a graphic designer. He has to know how to create a presentation that works visually *and* technically, suits the site content, meets web usability and accessibility standards, and is attractive to search engines. He also has to have an understanding of business.

BOX 3.2 Website copyright

Who owns the copyright to a website? Unless otherwise agreed at the outset, the web development agency has the copyright to the presentation and the code of a website (not the content). Some agencies, however, will give the client copyright to the presentation, if the presentation was created specifically for that client.

If you want to move to a new agency, the agency that built the site might ask you to pay for the code before letting you take the site elsewhere. This is likely if the site has been built recently. If it is several years old, however, the agency is unlikely to have any use for the code, as it will be too dated, and will probably not ask for payment.

When you have your initial discussions with a web development agency, you should ask what the copyright situation is. For more information on copyright and websites, it's worth taking a look at www.netmag.co.uk/zine/design-culture/copyright-for-web-designers

Presentation concept and elements

From the overall presentation concept to the many elements that make up that presentation, simplicity should reign supreme. Cluttered concepts produce cluttered pages, and cluttered pages put off potential customers.

When starting to think about the concept, the first thing the web designer needs to do is to see what category the website falls into. Then he looks at the objectives of the site in order to determine the message that the site needs to deliver, as well as at competitors' sites to see what they look like. Once he has done this, he starts designing a presentation that reflects both the purpose and personality of the business.

Having established the concept, it's necessary to translate it into the elements that make up the presentation – size, layout, typeface, colours and images.

BOX 3.3 Deciding on the presentation concept

When our client with the idea for the 'talking cards' website asked us to develop their site, having established that there was a market for the product (see Box 2.1), we held a brainstorming session with them to determine the presentation concept. This involved talking about their passion, their product and their objectives, and then coming up with about 30 words that could be attached to the venture.

Through further discussion we were able to encapsulate the venture in two sentences, and a company ethos and personality began to emerge. This enabled us to start thinking about branding and images. A week later, when we had all had time to think in detail about what had come out of the brainstorming session, we met again and were able to finalise the concept and ask the designer to produce a draft presentation.

If you look at a website page, what do you see?

- Does the page fit your screen?
- How are the text and images on the page arranged?
- Is the typeface easy to read?
- What are the dominant colours and do they complement each other?
- Are there photos and graphics and, if so, are they static or moving?

A visitor to your site will scan, absorb and assess all these elements, separately and as a whole. Similarly, a designer produces the presentation by creating each element in its own right and within the context of the overall concept.

Size

How wide should a website page be? Should it be 'fluid' ('dynamic'; i.e., expand to the width of a visitor's window) or 'fixed' ('static'; i.e., be a specified width, whatever the window size; see Figure 3.3, page 34)? There are pros and cons of both approaches.

For example, 'fixed' is easier to create and control, but doesn't scale well, whereas 'fluid' caters for ever-improving screen resolutions and new platforms such as PDAs (personal digital assistants, e.g., Blackberry, Treo and iPhone), but can result in a distorted presentation and text lines that are too long. The eye has difficulty reading lines longer than about 14 words (or 12 cm), whether on paper or on screen. In addition, a fundamental rule of website presentation is that visitors should never have to scroll horizontally across a page to read the text.

How long should a website page be? The rule of thumb is that visitors should not have to scroll down more than another page and a third beyond the page they first see on their screen. The reason is simple – visitors get annoyed, or lost, or both, if they have to scroll down a very long page and / or jump to and fro between the links on a long

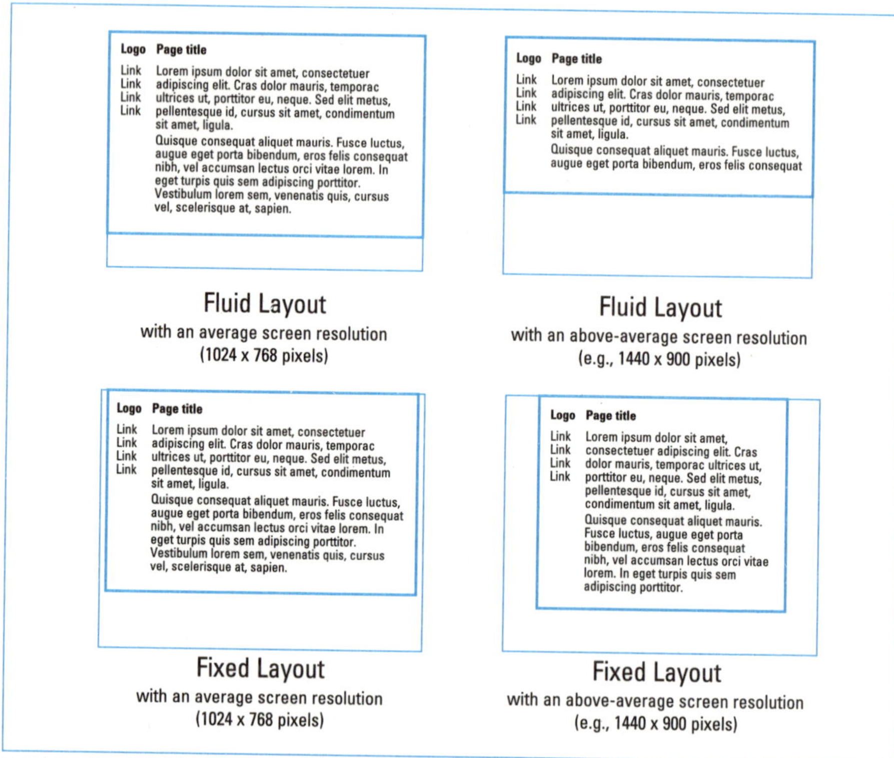

FIGURE 3.3 Fixed and fluid websites

When deciding whether a website should be fixed or fluid, the main question is: Who are your visitors? Are they likely to have the latest computer hardware and software, or do they vary considerably in the hardware and software they can access? With a fixed layout, if the window is smaller than the web page grid, horizontal scrolling can occur (poor practice). Fixed layouts are common for corporate sites, where the main objective is to provide information, and the branding (logo size, etc.) is important. With a fluid layout, the website resizes and adapts itself to various window sizes, often with unpredictable results. Fluid layouts are common for e-commerce websites, where space is important.

page. It's better, anyway, to create a new page with its own URL than to try to fit too much onto one page. A new page means a new URL, and a new URL means more for search engines to look at. And while I'm on the subject of scrolling, always avoid the use of internal scrolling (see Figure 3.4).

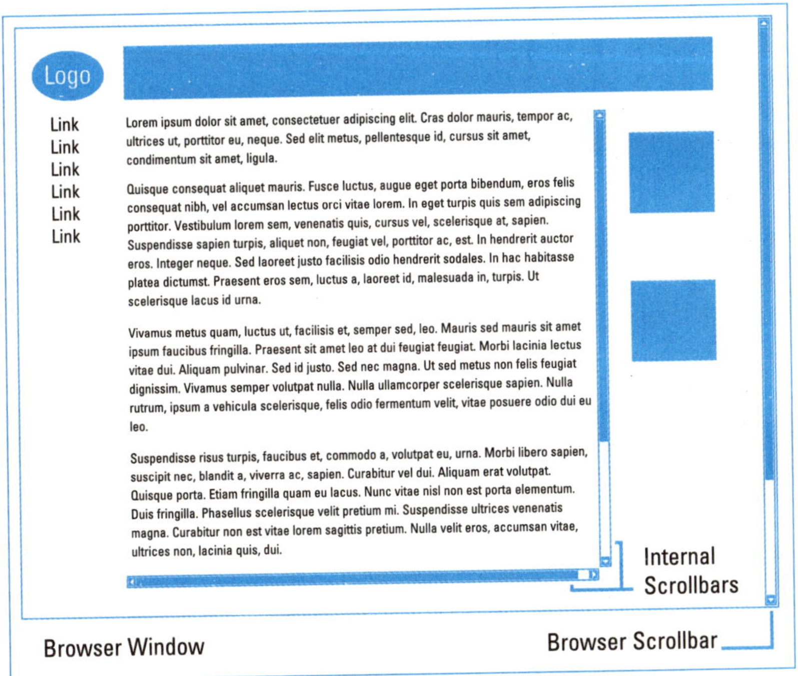

FIGURE 3.4 Internal scrollbars – not recommended

It is not a good idea to create web pages with internal scrolling (vertical and/or horizontal scrollbars within the page, in addition to the usual browser scrollbar at the right-hand side of pages). Internal scrolling can confuse the visitor, especially if the window is small and the screen resolution low.

Having said all that, there is a case for long pages in some instances, and the scroll wheel on a mouse makes scrolling easy and more acceptable these days. Many sites now do have long pages where it's better for visitors to be able to read and print out a long article with one click than to have to click through several pages.

Layout

'Layout' means the arrangement of page features (e.g., headings, text, photos, videos, advertisements, captions, navigation bars, search boxes, links, feeds, downloads). Again, the key here is simplicity. The simpler the layout, the easier the page will be for the visitor to scan and explore.

The main principles of website page layout are:

- space (preferably white or neutrally coloured, but see 'Colour', page 39)
- balance (careful arrangement of page features either symmetrically or asymmetrically)
- consistency (coherence and logicality in the use and alignment of page features)
- contrast (using presentation elements to reinforce hierarchy, focal points, key features, etc.)
- proximity (grouping related information)
- rhythm (repeating or alternating page features to create unity and movement)

Deliberately, 'space' heads this list. It is the most important ingredient in good website layout. Reading on screen isn't easy. The more space there is on a page, the easier it is on the eye and therefore the more comfortable visitors will feel exploring your site. So do make sure that your site has plenty of space around and between all the page features (see Figure 3.5).

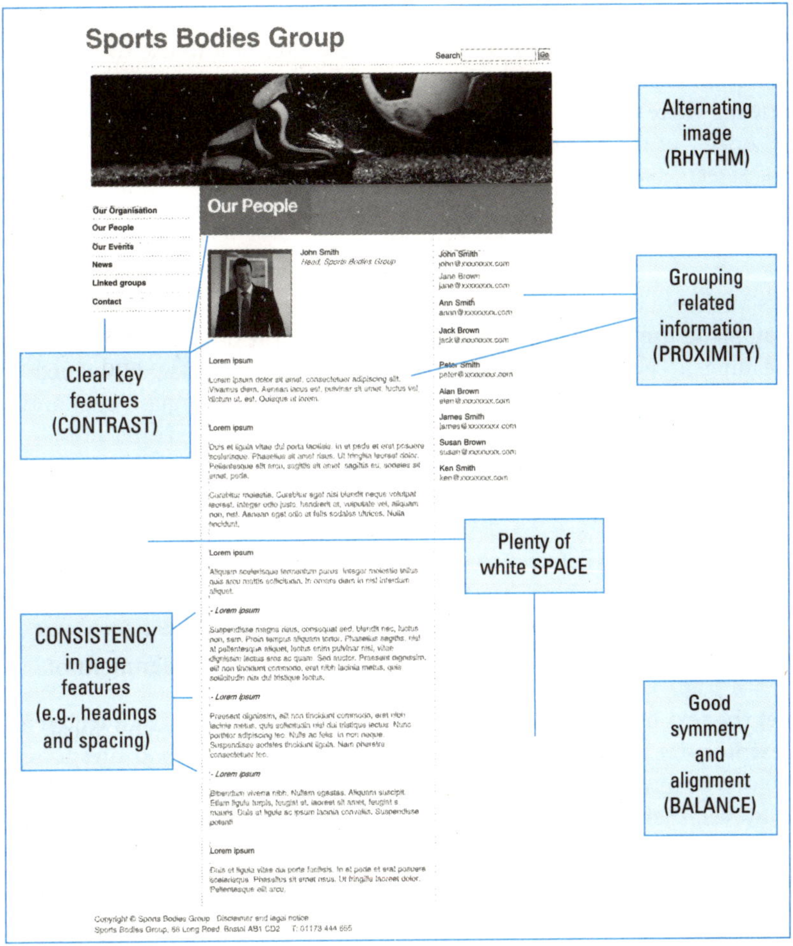

FIGURE 3.5 The main principles of website page layout

Ensuring that web pages reflect the principles of page layout will give your website a professional look and make the information it carries easy to scan, read and absorb.

Typefaces

What typefaces should be used on a website? It's best to use the common typefaces that all browsers recognise and are most readable on screen. There are two groups of typefaces: *serif* (i.e., with curls or lines – 'serifs' – at the end of letters) and *sans serif* (i.e., with no serifs). On the screen, *sans serif* typefaces are easier to read (letters are less clearly defined on screen than on a printed page, and *serif* typefaces can look a bit blurred on some screen displays).

It's advisable to put your main text in a *sans serif* typeface; for contrast, you could use a *serif* typeface for short pieces of text (e.g., captions, headings). The most common *sans serif* typefaces are Arial, Trebuchet and Verdana. The most common *serif* typefaces are Georgia, Times and Times New Roman. Avoid using more than two typefaces on a site. Many successful sites have only one *sans serif* typeface, using different sizes and colours to provide the contrast (see Box 3.4).

Don't make the typeface size for the main text too small or too large – 10 or 11 points is best. (Developers often talk in terms of 'ems' or 'percentages' when it comes to type size, because 'point' is a fixed size but 'ems' / 'percentages' are relative to the browser settings.)

Let the text breathe by having generous 'leading' (the space in which a text line sits, also measured in points). It's common on good sites to see 10 or 11 point text on 13 or 14 point leading, respectively. Remember, however, that typeface sizes vary (e.g., 11 point Times is smaller than 11 point Arial or Georgia), so draft page designs should always use the typeface that will be used ultimately, not an interim typeface. A good designer will also use a process called 'anti-aliasing' when there is text on an image; it smoothes jagged edges, and is especially important when a site is likely to be read on low-resolution screens.

Be consistent in the use of **bold** and *italic*. Try not to use too much of either, as this can give website text a cluttered look. Also, avoid

BOX 3.4 Choosing readable typefaces

Here are some examples of typefaces that are suitable for websites because they are browser-friendly and are clear and readable on screen. Two of them, Georgia and Verdana, were specially created for the screen.

It's best to use *sans serif* typefaces for the main text, and either a *serif* or *sans serif* typeface (if you're looking for contrast) for the short pieces of text, such as headings and image captions.

Sans serif

Arial	The quick brown fox jumps over the lazy dog
Trebuchet	The quick brown fox jumps over the lazy dog
Verdana	The quick brown fox jumps over the lazy dog

Serif

Georgia	The quick brown fox jumps over the lazy dog
Times	The quick brown fox jumps over the lazy dog
Times New Roman	The quick brown fox jumps over the lazy dog

'The quick brown fox jumps over the lazy dog' is the sentence commonly used to test typefaces because it includes all the letters of the alphabet.

using capital letters (caps) in text – they make visitors feel that you're shouting at them! Statistics show that using caps reduces readability by about 10%.

Colour

The key to good colour use on a website is subtlety. Soft light-to-medium colours usually work better than bold dark colours (unless bold colours are used sparingly, or you deliberately want a bold, dark image, see Figure 3.6, colour page III).

A palette of no more than three colours is best. The selected colours should:

- pick up on the business brand colour(s)
- complement the site content rather than dominate it
- work well together (e.g., blue and beige work well, but blue and yellow do not)
- reinforce contrast between page features (such as text and background; see Box 3.5)
- be suitable for denoting site functions (e.g., for 'mouseovers' – text links highlighted by the mouse cursor; use the same colour for these links throughout the site)
- be used for separating different areas of a page or types of information (e.g., white background for main text, light coloured background for secondary text such as captions and news items)

BOX 3.5 Choosing text colours

When it comes to choosing the colour of your text and its background, leading the pack by a mile is black text on a white background. The worst (most unreadable) choice is red text on a black background. So, from best to worst:

BEST	black text on a white background
↓	blue text on a white background
	black text on a grey background
	grey text on a white background
	red text on a blue background
WORST	red text on a black background

Avoid white text on any background. The darker background colour 'seeps' into the white letters and casts a shadow over them, making the text difficult to read.

Avoid 'busy' backgrounds. Too many colours and images behind text get in the way of the text and its message, and give the page a cluttered look.

Some sites use only one colour, in various shades. Done professionally, this can be very effective, giving a website texture and style.

Images

The term 'images' in the context of website presentation means graphics (e.g., buttons, diagrams, drawings, graphs, icons, logos and menu bars), still photos and moving images (e.g., animation, videos). Using images as decoration is fine, as long as it's not overdone. Most images used in the text, however, should have a clear purpose – to convey information more quickly and effectively than words could do.

There are three types of image formats that can be used on the web: JPEG (Joint Photographic Experts Group), PNG (Portable Network Graphic) and GIF (Graphic Interchange Format). GIFs are restricted to 256 colours, but can be viewed on all computers and by all browsers. PNGs were created to improve upon and replace GIFs. JPEGs are the most popular because they are higher quality images and have more than 256 colours (see Chapter 5, Figure 5.7); most computers can handle JPEGs. So PNGs and GIFs tend to be used for graphics, whereas JPEGs are used for still photos.

Graphics and still photos can enhance the look of a website, but should be used carefully and consistently. Poorly used, they give the site a cluttered appearance, reduce the download speed and can create problems for special needs visitors. It's also important to remember that the resolution of images on the screen (usually 72 dpi) is always poorer than on the printed page (usuall, 300 dpi), so too many images makes it hard on the eye. With still photos, the original image should be as crisp and clear as possible, so that it still looks good when enlarged on the screen.

Creating moving images involves using a range of applications, the most common ones being Flash (high quality; see Box 3.6, page 42) and

BOX 3.6 Using Flash

Adobe Flash, usually referred to simply as Flash, is a powerful animation tool for creating dynamic content on websites, but like every tool in a developer's toolbox, it should be handled with care. Some sites suit Flash, others don't.

Flash is good to use for:

- advertisement banners
- animation and cartoons
- games
- live communication
- multimedia sites
- training and distance learning
- videos

Used effectively, Flash produces high-quality images, is browser friendly and can have a positive effective on how users interact wth your site. But remember that it also takes up space, can cause accessibility problems (although this is improving), does not attract search engines and can distract and annoy visitors.

Flash has become popular as a video-streaming tool. Before the arrival of video phones, digital cameras and video-sharing websites such as YouTube, people wanting to add video clips to their websites had to go through a difficult encoding process and had to solve hosting issues relating to heavy files. Today, being able to shoot videos digitally allows people to upload files directly onto free hosting services, such as YouTube.

Created in 2005, YouTube uses Flash technology to display user-generated video content. It also generates HTML code that you can paste onto a website page to allow you to embed video clips on your site. Statistics published by *The Wall Street Journal* show that in 2006 YouTube was hosting about 6.1 million videos and had 500,000 user accounts; by April 2008 these figures had climbed to 83.4 million videos and 3.75 million user accounts.

animated GIFs (easy to create, but can give a site a rather downmarket look). Moving images should be used only if they enhance a visitor's experience, and then only once on a page, if possible; more than this could distract the visitor. Using Flash for opening pages or as a recurring presentation feature is not recommended – it's annoying, distracting and outmoded, and can obstruct searches through the content. The same goes for music – don't use it unless the site is specifically about music.

Standardised presentation format

Over the past few years the arrangement of the main features on a website page has become fairly standardised. This is partly to make it easier for visitors to scan and navigate a site – people are more comfortable with the familiar, and the more familiar the presentation of a website page, the quicker they'll find what they're looking for. It's also partly because we now know far more about how people scan a website page.

BOX 3.7 A presentation checklist

When thinking about website presentation, it's a good idea to look at the home pages of some top international companies (who can afford the very best designers) and analyse their design elements. For example:

- Does the design reflect the company ethos and purpose?
- Is the format fixed or fluid?
- Is there no (or limited) scrolling?
- Does the site have a feeling of spaciousness?
- Is the main background colour neutral?
- Are there clear focal points on the page?
- Is there a recognisable 'theme' to the layout?
- Is the text easy to read?
- Do the colour combinations work?
- Is Flash used and, if so, what for?

Research on eye movements across a screen has shown that:

- visitors tend to look first at the top left of the screen (so who you are – your name, logo, etc. – is best placed here), and then across the top of the screen
- they then scan down the left side and into the centre of the page (so your main message should be in the middle of the screen)
- they pay more attention to the left side of a page than to the right (so align headings and text to the left; use the left and centre of the page for important items, and the right side for secondary items)
- the less the eye has to move horizontally the better (so dividing text into columns is a good idea)
- the eye is confused by distorted letter and word spacing in a line of text, so align text on the left, with a 'ragged' right edge ('unjustified' text); avoid centred text; and separate paragraphs by a line space rather than indenting the first line of each new paragraph)

Typically, a website home page:

- carries the branding (logo, etc.) across the top (or top left) of the page
- has a search facility at the top right, often near the contact details
- has a customer or community login facility top right
- has a site map accessed by an icon bottom left or right
- has a horizontal navigation bar, with a limited number of items, near the top of the page
- is based on a two- or three-column (vertical) format
- uses the left column to list the site's main categories, linking visitors to the rest of the site
- uses the central column(s) to carry the main messages (in text and images)
- uses the right column to carry links to miscellaneous features (e.g., newsfeeds, endorsements)

Figure 3.7 illustrates the layout of a typical business website home page (in this case the website of a book publisher), based on the standardised

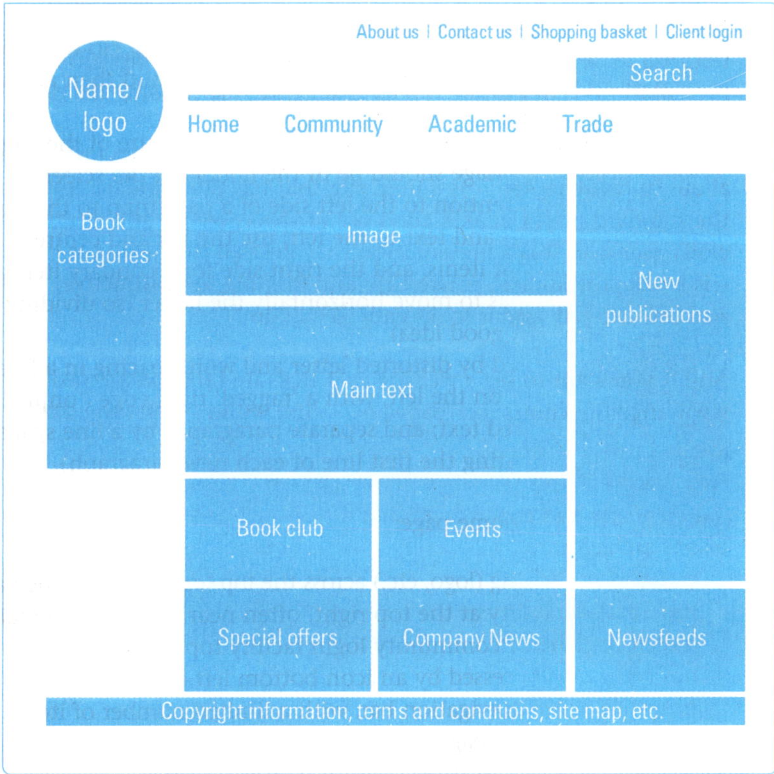

FIGURE 3.7 Standardised presentation format

Although the presentation format of a typical business website has become fairly standardised, you don't have to stick to it rigidly, but whatever changes you make the most important thing to bear in mind is what suits the visitor (as shown in this format for a book publisher's website). If visitors are used to seeing the shopping basket top right, why put it somewhere else and make them look for it? Similarly, if (as research shows) they tend to look first at the top left of the page, then it makes sense to put your most important information (name, logo and product categories) there.

format. You don't have to stick rigidly to this type of arrangement, of course, but it is research based and it has proved successful. There's nothing to be gained – except visitors' exasperation – from creating presentations that deviate too far from what has become the norm.

Figure 3.8 (see colour page IV) illustrates all the elements I have talked about in this chapter. It is a fluid site that has the standard features in the standard places, makes good use of space, colour and images, and is easily scanned. It is a presentation that ticks all the boxes for the visitor – it looks professional, interesting and inviting, it is attractive, clean and uncluttered, and it looks easy to explore.

And if you want to see a website that ticks no boxes at all, take a look at www.angelfire.com/super/badwebs/ – 'the world's worst website'!

Chapter 4

CONTENT

IN THE ONLINE WORLD, content is king. Presentation is important, architecture is essential, but what matters most on any website – what will get your website noticed – is content. Good content attracts search engines, and search engines give you visibility, and visibility brings potential customers.

What does 'content' mean? Words. All the words on a website, from the words in the text on the website pages and those in its information sources (e.g., advertisements, blogs, documents, endorsements, e-newsletters, forums, newsfeeds, press releases and reviews) to the words in the tags at the top and bottom of pages, in the incoming links to the site and in the URLs of each website page.

Getting the words right is crucial. They should:

- suit the context – a website
- be written with two audiences in mind – your target customers and the search engines

These factors determine who writes the words, what words are used, how many are used and how they are arranged. This chapter looks at how writing for the web differs from writing for other media, and then at how to make text attractive to both visitors and search engines.

Writing for a website

A website is a flexible and interactive medium intended to deliver information concisely and quickly. Writing words (copy) for a website differs greatly from writing words for static, one-way media such as a printed books, magazines or newspapers. A website copywriter needs to take these differences into account:

- a website doesn't have a finite number of pages – new ones can be added and old ones removed at any time

- it doesn't have a publication date – visitors expect it to be up to date
- it doesn't have a beginning, middle or end (the home page is a sort of beginning, but it's not necessarily the first page that visitors see)
- visitors can usually see only one page at a time
- each page carries information telling visitors what's on other pages and how to get there
- visitors use links to move from one page to another on a site, often in a non-linear way
- they often scan – rather than read – website pages
- they expect to find the information they're looking for quickly
- they expect to be able to interact with the website

What do these differences mean? They mean that a website is not the place for ambiguity, inflexibility, waffle, sloppy structure or careless presentation. Many websites fail because they are guilty of some or all of these sins. If website text is to succeed in attracting visitors and search engines, it should be written by a professional copywriter to ensure that it is:

- clear
- concise
- compelling

Add 'adaptable', 'easily scanned' 'informative', 'persuasively presented' and 'extremely well organised' – and you will be well on the way to creating a website that will generate more business.

Writing for the visitor

All writing has a purpose. Good writing achieves its purpose. The purpose of the text on an e-commerce website is to persuade visitors to stay on the site for as long as it takes to convert them from visitors into customers. How is this achieved?

Foundations

The first thing to do is to get the foundations right. These include:

- *grammar:* 'grammar' means the system of rules describing the function of words (e.g., adjectives, verbs, nouns) and how to combine words to form phrases, clauses and sentences; make sure that, for the person writing the text, the definition of a pronoun or the rules of sentence are not just distant memories

BOX 4.1 Getting the foundations right

Don't rely on the spell-checker to highlight spelling mistakes. You could end up providing copy which carries embarrassing mistakes that a spell-checker would not have picked up. Here are the sort of mistakes a spell-checker would not find:

> Our lawyers charge a nominal fee for the initial daft contract.
>
> Instead of a fortnight in New York, why not have a wee in Washington?
>
> She has taken up her new position in pubic affairs.
>
> We have organised some trails of our new system.
>
> Pensioners on a low income are finding it hard to exit.

Poor grammar and punctuation can lead to ambiguity. Website visitors don't want to waste time working out what the text means. Here is what can happen when sentences are carelessly constructed and commas misplaced:

> No one was injured in the blast, which was attributed to a build-up of gas by one town official.
>
> The employee talked about his co-worker who was killed in an interview with Barbara Williams.
>
> The summary of information contains totals of the number of students broken down by sex, marital status and age.
>
> Drunk gets nine months in violin case.

- *spelling:* spelling mistakes imply laziness and could lead visitors to question your overall reliability and professionalism; with a dictionary handy, there's no excuse for spelling mistakes (don't rely on spell-checkers, they can lead to embarrassing mistakes; see Box 4.1)

- *punctuation:* many websites have a rather random approach to punctuation (e.g., commas and apostrophes in the wrong place; colons used instead of semi-colons; hyphens used instead of dashes; and exclamation marks all over the place); poor punctuation will make your readers stumble, and if they stumble once too often they'll leave your site

- *vocabulary:* choosing the right words is important, not least because it means visitors won't stumble over the text; it's common – and annoying – to see wrong words used on websites (e.g., 'affect' instead of 'effect', 'ascribe' / 'subscribe', 'militate' / 'mitigate', 'systemic' / 'systematic'); also, use what has become standard web vocabulary where it exists (e.g., 'shopping basket', not 'shopping bag')

Dos and don'ts

The basic rules of good writing for the web include using:

- short words and phrases rather than their longer equivalents (e.g., 'start' instead of 'commence'; 'tell' / 'inform'; 'about' / 'in connection with'; 'although' / 'despite the fact that'
- short sentences (but vary their length to give the text rhythm, one of the secrets of compelling writing)
- short paragraphs (preferably no more than three sentences long, or about 35 words)
- headings and subheadings (at least two or three on a page); this makes it easier to scan the page

BOX 4.2 Compiling copy for a website

When compiling the text for an e-commerce website, where does a copywriter start? Usually, the process follows these steps:

1. Obtain information on the company by, for example, interviewing relevant staff and looking at company products and documents
2. Produce a draft structure of the text, showing the main categories of information to be covered
3. Revise this structure through discussions with company staff responsible for the site and with the web development agency building the site
4. Produce a visual diagram of the site content pages, prioritised (see Figure 4.1, page 54)
5. When everyone has approved this structure, conduct a keyword analysis (see Chapter 6) and start writing the text for each page, incorporating the keywords and bearing in mind all the dos and don'ts listed in this chapter
6. Submit this first draft to the company and then, after making any necessary revisions, submit it as final copy to the web developer
7. When the site has been built and the text is all in place, proofread it not only for spelling and punctuation mistakes, but also for such things as word breaks at the end of lines, the size and spacing of headings, and typeface size and leading

- positive rather than negative sentences where possible (e.g., 'Items bought before 30 May will come with a gift', not 'Items bought after 30 May will not come with a gift')
- the active rather than the passive voice (e.g., 'We hold networking breakfasts each Tuesday', not 'Networking breakfasts are held each Tuesday')
- as few words as possible, with every word having a purpose and none being redundant
- a conversational, but not too informal, tone (e.g., using 'you' makes visitors feel they are part of a dialogue, and not simply having information thrown at them)
- lists where appropriate – they make scanning easy

Copywriters should avoid:

- using clichés, jargon, slang and worn-out old expressions (e.g., 'going forward', 'mission-oriented marketing', 'pushing the envelope' and 'thinking outside the box')
- using acronyms unless visitors will almost certainly be more familiar with them than the full meaning (e.g., there's no need to spell out BBC, HTML or NATO)
- using too many adjectives and adverbs
- proofreading on screen; it's better to read, spot mistakes and amend text on paper, so print the document out to proofread it

Organisation

How will the copywriter organise the information on your site? Bearing in mind that, initially, visitors scan rather than read site pages, it's necessary to spend a lot of time thinking about content organisation. It involves planning, liaison and clear thinking. The key factors in organising site content are categorisation, hierarchy and navigation:

- *Categorisation:* How site content is categorised depends on what your message is and how you think visitors will use the site. For the main text, options include categorising by topic, theme, function, user group, region, or a mixture of these (a mixture might give visitors more options, or more ways of finding the same information). When deciding on the number of categories (and subcategories), do allow for the growth of the site and the possible need to add more categories. For secondary text (e.g., blogs, newsletters, PDF downloads), take care to make it distinct from the main text.

- *Hierarchy:* The main text should move naturally from the general (brief introductory texts) to the specific (more detailed texts). This can be achieved through the use of headings, subheadings and links, conveying a sense of progress. One-line, attention-grabbing headings and subheadings make page scanning easy, and they should work as a set by using the same phraseology.

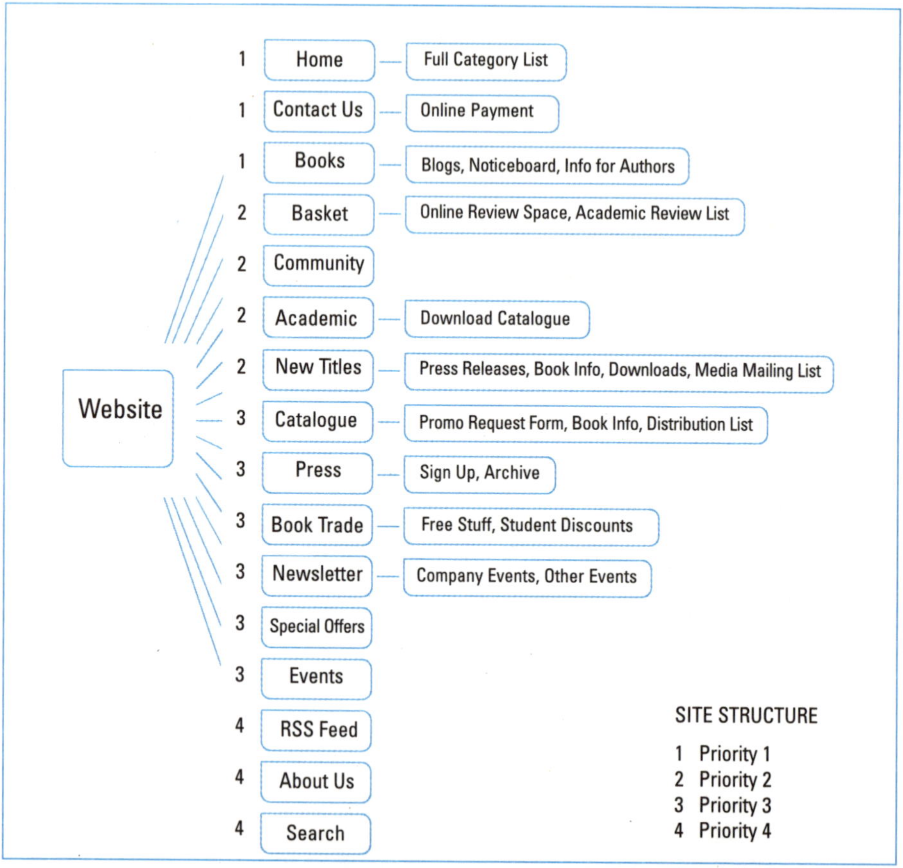

FIGURE 4.1 Categorising and prioritising site pages

This diagrammatic example of site structure (based on the content preparation for a publisher's website; see also Figure 7.3) makes it clear for all concerned – client (publisher), copywriter, developer, designer – which pages take priority and which are of secondary importance. A hallmark of sites lacking this basic content categorisation and prioritisation is poor navigation.

- *Navigation:* Visitors should be able to move logically and seamlessly across the site, from category to subcategory, from the general to the specific, and back again, using one or more of the following navigation tools: text links (e.g., in navigation bars and embedded in the text); iconic links (e.g., via photos, icons and buttons); search facility (i.e., using the search box); and the site map (see Chapter 5).

If the copywriter gets the foundations right, adheres to the dos and don'ts listed earlier, and takes care over content organisation, the visitor will find a site that:

- is easily scanned, informative and concise, with no words out of place or redundant
- says clearly, via the main text and headings, what the site offers
- shows clearly, via the navigation tools, how to find what the site offers
- shows, via fresh content (e.g., newsfeeds, blogs) and interactive facilities (e.g., forums, customer login areas), that it is regularly updated and values visitor interaction

Writing for the search engines

If you want to increase site traffic and revenue, you have to make it easy for potential customers to find you. So the nearer your site is to the top of the organic listings, the better. But you don't get there by chance. It takes a lot of thought, planning and skill on the part of website developers and copywriters to get a site onto the first page of the listings. It is all part of search engine optimisation (SEO) – one of the most important factors in creating a successful website.

In Chapter 5, I look at SEO from the developer's point of view and in Chapter 6 there is an overview of SEO. Here, the focus is on SEO from the copywriter's point of view.

Keywords

What words might potential customers enter in a search box when they're looking for the sort of products you offer? To compile a list of possible keywords, the copywriter should liaise with both the web developer and the company, as well as asking colleagues and customers for suggestions.

Whittling the list down to about 20 phrases and then running an analysis report on it will reveal the words most likely to bring people to the site (see Chapter 6, Figure 6.3). The developer needs to incorporate them into the site's HTML code (e.g., for the title and meta tags and alt attributes, all unseen by visitors, but very important to search engines).

The copywriter needs to embed the keywords into:

- headings and subheadings (coded H1 and H2, respectively; search engines pay a lot of attention to headings, so make them meaningful and as keyword-rich as possible)

BOX 4.3 Choosing keywords carefully

A travel company had had a website for several years that wasn't getting much traffic. They covered much of the Middle East and their target group seemed fairly broad. When we discussed their business in detail with them, however, the focus seemed to be on the Yemen and upmarket clients. So we suggested aiming at a niche market place by giving the site an upmarket appearance and selecting niche, upmarket keywords.

The company researched the sites of other upmarket travel companies to get an idea of the sort of keywords to use, and these were incorporated into the new site. Gone were the rather broad and bland keywords used on the old site: 'Middle East', 'holidays', 'travel', 'adventure'. Instead, in came 'Yemen', 'discerning', 'tailor-made', 'individually crafted' and 'luxury'. With this, and some additional SEO work that we carried out, their website traffic doubled in just a few months.

- text (preferably the text near the top and bottom of a page, as this is where search engines look most; about three keywords per page)
- text links (see below)

Any changes to the selected keywords to improve the site ranking will be picked up by search engines and the relevant pages re-indexed.

Links

Search engines like text links (also called 'hypertext links'). It was common until few years ago to use 'Click here' to link one piece of text to another, and website texts were littered with 'Click here'. This is a waste of words and space. It's better to embed a link word into the text and use a 'mouseover' (see Figure 4.2, page 58).

Here are some other points to bear in mind with embedded text links:

- it should be clear, from the link words used, what they are likely to link to
- link words should reflect, as far as possible, the words or phrase they are linking to (e.g., if the link is to a page headed 'Product Description', the embedded link words should be 'product description', not 'description of product' or 'product specification')
- visitors and search engines are more likely to pick up a link word if it is placed at the end of a sentence or paragraph
- there shouldn't be too many link words on a page; text cluttered with links can be off-putting for visitors and search engines
- text links should be used to keep pages short (i.e., instead crowding a page with information on a particular topic, it's better to have summaries of information that use text links to take the visitor to more detailed information on secondary pages)

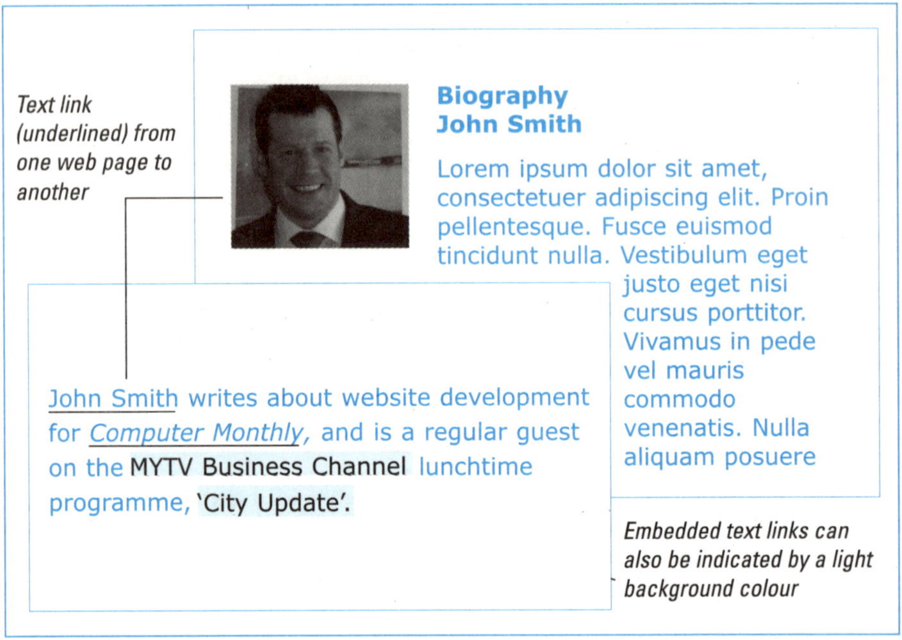

FIGURE 4.2 Embedding links in text

It's better to embed links in the text, as in this example, than to add 'Click here' to the text, which takes up valuable space and does not attract the search engines. Text links show up better with a 'mouseover' (i.e., when a mouse pointer goes over a word and brings up an underline below the word or a light background colour behind the word – now both familiar indications of a text link).

A note on the Latin text in this figure. This is the standard dummy text used by page designers (in both the print and website worlds) to show text placement, typeface and size, before the actual text is available. 'Lorem ipsum' was first used as dummy text in the 1500s, when a printer took a galley of type and scrambled it to make a specimen book. So if a web development agency presents you with a sample design that includes Latin text, don't be alarmed – but do insist on seeing the actual text as early in the development process as feasible.

New content

Search engines like new content. It shows them that the website is being kept up to date and gives them fresh material to look at and index. Sites that might be first class in many ways, but sit there doing nothing, will, after a while, start dropping down the search engine listings.

Whatever your business, there are many ways in which you can add new content to keep your site looking fresh and, above all, attractive to search engines. These include, in order of priority:

- new web pages
- press releases
- newsfeeds
- product reviews and recommendations
- blogs
- e-newsletters
- discussion forums
- advertisements

It's also a good idea to have forms on the site, where appropriate. They encourage interaction with visitors and make the site look active and busy, which search engines will notice. Keep forms short, simple and well targeted; don't make visitors fill in too much information or supply information that they can't see the point of. There are two good examples of forms in Figure 4.3 (page 60).

Creating the content for a website means serving many masters. You need to take account of what visitors want to see, what search engines find attractive, what the company wants to say and what the web designer and developer want to create.

And there is a sixth master – the written word; if you use it with care and respect, it will pay you great dividends.

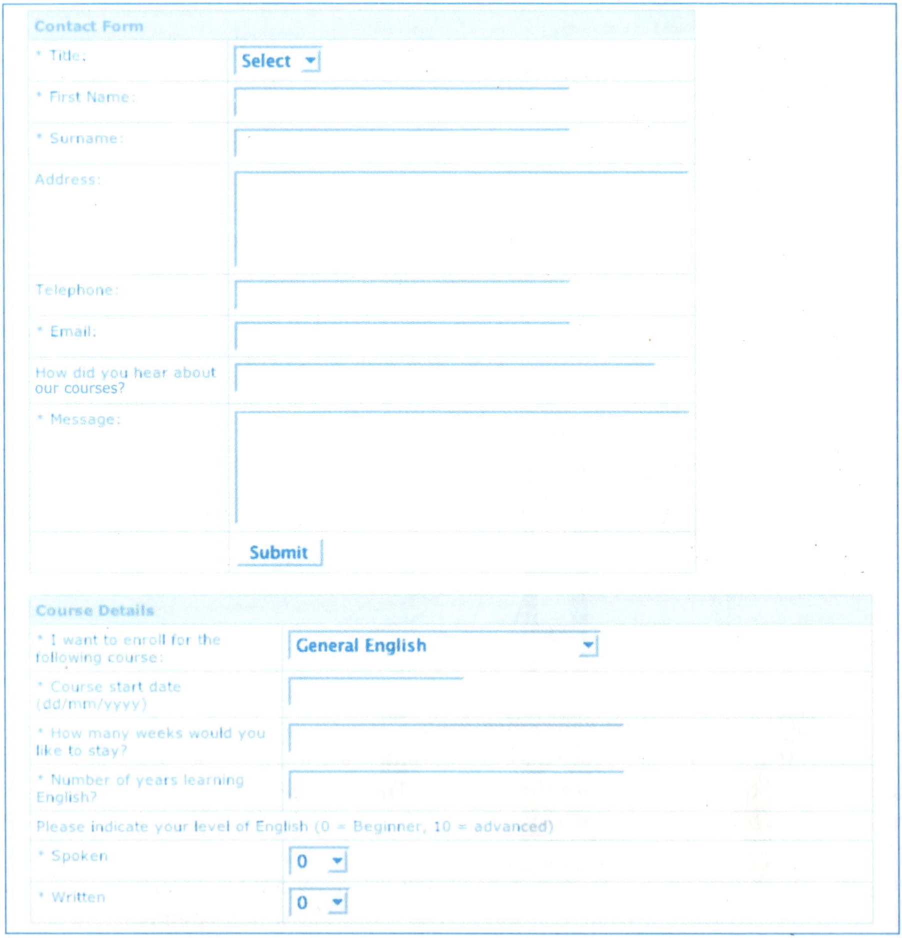

Contact Form

* Title: Select

* First Name:

* Surname:

Address:

Telephone:

* Email:

How did you hear about our courses?

* Message:

Submit

Course Details

* I want to enroll for the following course: General English

* Course start date (dd/mm/yyyy)

* How many weeks would you like to stay?

* Number of years learning English?

Please indicate your level of English (0 = Beginner, 10 = advanced)

* Spoken 0

* Written 0

FIGURE 4.3 Keeping forms simple and targeted

Forms are a good way to foster interaction, which helps make a site feel busy and active. Try to keep forms short, clear, logical and simple, and don't ask for more information than you need.

Chapter 5

ARCHITECTURE

MOST OF WHAT YOU'VE read in this book so far would have been familiar or easily understood. It's stuff that you've probably dealt with before (e.g., prioritising objectives, identifying customers, assessing competitors) or that you've seen on a computer screen (e.g., the words and layout of a business website).

Now you've got to the bit that's less visible and, probably, a lot less familiar. And if that wasn't bad enough, it's the bit that's piled high with acronyms. We're talking about 'information architecture'. In website development, this is the term used to describe how information is organised and labelled on a site, and how visitors navigate their way through it to get to what they want (see Box 5.1).

This chapter looks at what goes into building the information architecture and developing the navigation system, taking into account two aspects of this process that are crucial to a successful site – *accessibility* and *usability*. It then examines the four basic components of site architecture:

- the mark-up languages (e.g., HTML, XHTML and XML) that determine the *structure* of a web page
- the style sheet language (CSS) that determines its *presentation* (e.g., layout, typeface, colour)
- the server-side languages (e.g., PHP, ASP, JSP) that determine its *behaviour* (functionality)
- the database languages (e.g., SQL, MySQL) that store all the site *information* and send it out when a server-side language tells them to

Or, to put it another way: how it's built, what it looks like, what it does, and what it holds.

BOX 5.1 Defining 'information architecture'

The term 'information architecture' was coined in 1975 by an architect, Richard Wurman, who became interested in how information was gathered, organised and presented. He defined 'information architecture' as "organising the patterns in data, making the complex clear". The term then remained largely dormant in the computer world until 1996, when two library scientists, Lou Rosenfeld and Peter Morville, used it to define work they were doing on structuring websites and intranets. The Information Architecture Institute defines it as "the structural design of shared information environments".

BOX 5.2 Avoiding website jargon

The non-technical person shouldn't have found this book difficult to understand up to this point. Now it might get a bit difficult because we've moved into the world of computer terminology and jargon. People working in that world often find it difficult to explain the jargon they use.

If you've employed web developers to build a new site for you, particularly if it's an e-commerce site whose success or failure could have a great impact on your business, you must try to knock down any language barrier between you and the developer by insisting, from the outset, that they explain any terms you don't understand. And also ask them to explain exactly what your role is during site development, who has to sign off what and when, what feedback you're expected to give, and at what stages you can or can't make changes.

If you do all this, you'll get the best out of them, they'll get the best out of you, and your site will get the business you want.

The concluding part of the chapter outlines a series of measures that need to be integrated into the whole process of building the architecture to ensure that the site functions smoothly and that its e-commerce potential is maximised.

Building the foundations

Information architecture is the engine that makes everything you see on a computer screen look and function the way it does. When you have a clear idea of what information you want on your site – its content – and what you want it to do, work can start on laying the foundations for the site's information architecture. This involves:

1 Dividing the content into main categories and making a list of the site pages based on this category list (see Chapter 4)

2 Deciding what structural model to use; the most common one for e-commerce sites is a hierarchical model, starting with the home page, but there are many other options (see Figure 5.1)

3 Creating a visual diagram that is easily understood by all involved (developer, designer, copywriter and you, the client), showing the main site pages (prioritised), a note on the content of each page, and how each page links to the rest of the site (see Figures 4.1 and 7.3)

4 Defining the navigation system that will be used to link items within and between the site pages

5 Producing a design template – the presentation concept – showing the look, layout and main features of the site pages

6 Writing the detailed specifications (or 'blueprint') for the site, page by page; from these specifications and the design template, the developer builds the site using various computer languages to create the structure, presentation, behaviour and databases

Navigation

There are few things that are more likely to annoy potential customers visiting your site than poor navigation. If they encounter navigation

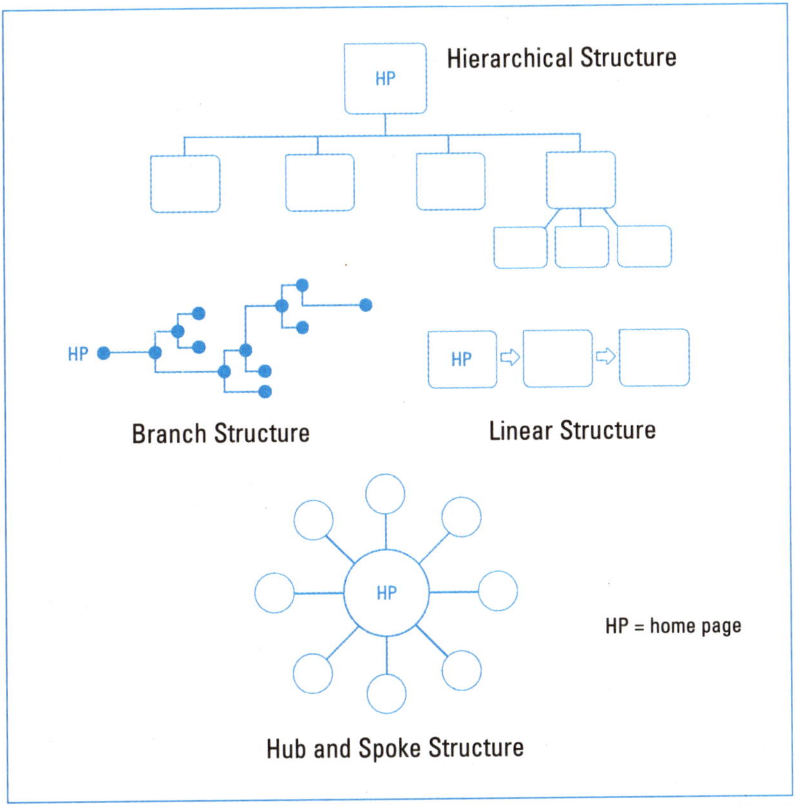

FIGURE 5.1 Choosing the organisational model

Websites can be built on the basis of a variety of models, such as those shown here. The hierarchical model is the most common one used for e-commerce sites.

problems when they are trying to find what they are looking for on the site, they'll leave it very quickly. And you will have lost the opportunity to generate business.

A site with good navigation means that, at any time, visitors can see where they are, where they've been, where they can go to next and how to get back again.

Site navigation is based on four types of links:

- *text links:* navigation bar items, drop-down lists, text-embedded links (e.g., mouseovers), text appendages (e.g., 'read more'), alt attributes (text descriptions of images) and breadcrumb trails (a restricted link tool in that it shows you where you are and can take you back to where you were, but you can't use it to move forward)

- *iconic links:* icons, tabs, buttons and images such as logos, photos and drawings (it's now common for the website logo to feature on every page and to be a link to the home page, making it easy for visitors landing elsewhere on the site to get to the home page)

- *site search:* the search box facility (this should allow visitors to search your whole site – and only your site; it provides an instant link to what the visitor wants to find, cutting out the need to consult indexes and category lists; it should always be prominent on a page)

- *site map:* the one-stop navigation facility (using text or a diagram or both), giving visitors a quick and easy way of seeing how to get to anywhere on the site; every website page should carry a text or iconic link to the site map, preferably somewhere along the bottom of the page

A good site navigation system uses all four types of links. It uses them in a consistent way (e.g., in the same formats, colours and locations) on each page. It ensures that each page has text links that take visitors to

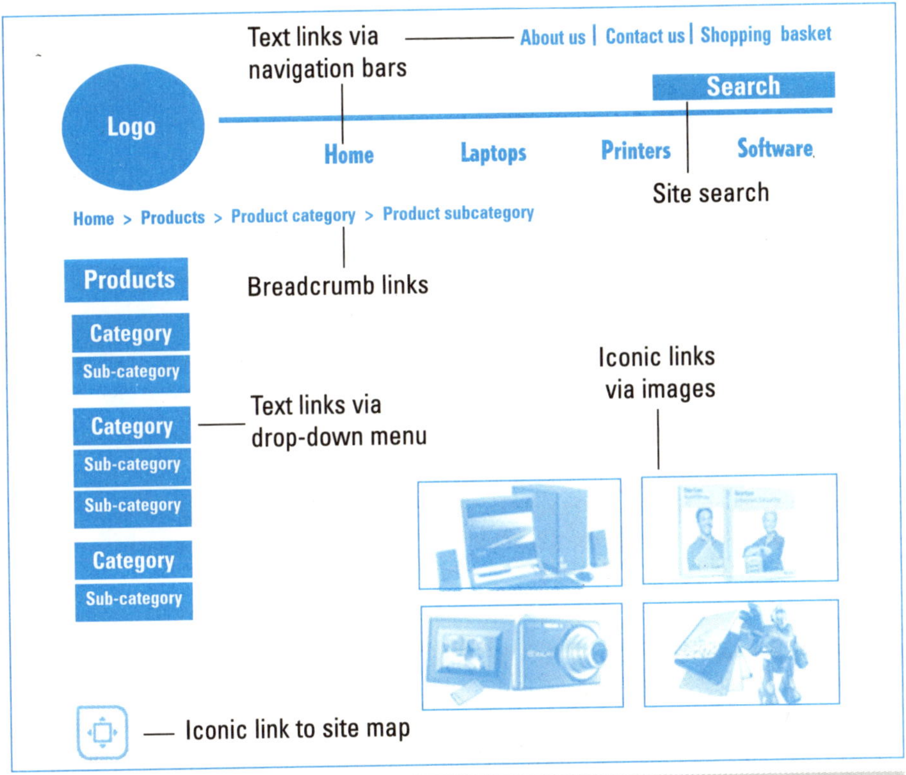

FIGURE 5.2 Site navigation links

Using a combination of text links, iconic links, the search facility and the site map, visitors should always be able to see – whatever page they're on – where they are, where they've been, where they can go to next and how to get back again.

all the major areas of the site, including the home page. And it is based on a logical progression from one item to another, requiring as few clicks as possible.

BOX 5.3 Navigation dos and don'ts

Here are some important dos and don'ts about site navigation:

- Site navigation should be logical and easy to follow
- Site pages shouldn't be overloaded with links, and links should be distinct from each other
- Text link appendages, if they have to be used, should be clear and short (e.g., 'read more' is better than 'for more information about this product')
- A mouseover link should change colour (or acquire an underline) when touched, to show that it is a link, and the colour used shouldn't make the text difficult to read
- It should be clear what the iconic links are linking to; users should never have to guess where a link is taking them
- It's common now for photos to be links, so there's no need to put 'click here' near them; just make sure they carry alt attributes, for the search engines (as noted in Chapter 3, there's no need for 'click here' at all – it wastes space)

Accessibility and usability

It's an exciting time to be building websites. Gone are the days of the 1990s when everything was browser led, but the browsers were at war with each other and so developers had to build sites in a multitude of configurations to suit different browsers (see Chapter 3, Figure 3.1). There were no rules or standards, and at every turn incompatibility seemed to frustrate the development of this new information medium.

Then, as you saw in Chapter 3, the W3C was set up and in the early 2000s things began to change. Rules were drawn up, standards were set, compatibility became an overriding goal, the browser wars ended and new computer languages gave new life to the medium. There were still some teething problems, but by about 2006 things had settled down, a sense of 'best practice' had kicked in and the internet had taken a great stride forward.

At the core of the W3C strategy to bring order to chaos are two fundamental tenets – *accessibility* and *usability*. If you want to maximise the potential of your website, adherence to W3C guidelines on accessibility and usability when building it is a must.

Accessibility

The term 'accessibility' in the context of websites means making sites accessible to as many people as possible, whether or not they are disabled and whatever device they're using (PCs, PDAs, mobile phones, etc.). Many people operate under constraints that the average able-bodied person living in an industrialised country knows little about.

For example, they might:

- be unable to see, hear, move or process some or any of the information on a site easily
- have difficulty reading or understanding text
- not have or be unable to use a keyboard or a mouse
- have a screen that is text-only, very small, black-and-white and / or low resolution
- have a slow and / or unreliable internet connection
- have an old browser, a voice browser or an old operating system

The number of people we're talking about here is substantial. Their desire to use the net is strong and the benefits they derive from it are significant. Why exclude them? It doesn't look good, morally, to build sites that they can't access, and it certainly doesn't make good business sense to do so. And building sites that work on some devices and not on others doesn't make business sense either.

There are three important additional factors to bear in mind about accessibility:

- in some countries website accessibility for disabled people is a legal requirement (e.g., in the UK, sites are seen as a public service and are bound by the Disabilities Discrimination Act [DDA])
- making websites accessible to as many people as possible also requires making them accessible to all current browsers

BOX 5.4 Creating an accessible site

Here are some of the things a website developer should do when building a site that will be accessible to as many people as possible:

- use style sheets (CSS) rather than HTML for site presentation; this makes it easier to provide text that is intelligible to most users, including people who use screen readers
- use CSS to reduce download time
- use text equivalents for non-text features such as photos (i.e., provide text descriptions – 'alt attributes' – of these features; in this way, people with sight problems are not excluded)
- ensure that text links make sense if they're read out of context (this is another good reason to avoid using 'Click here')
- use semantic mark-up language (i.e., the code – or mark-up language – should be written and structured in such a way as to be easily understood by browsers and search engines)
- validate the mark-up language (i.e., check that the code is correct by testing the site on http://validator.w3.org/)

These last two tasks are very important. If the code used isn't semantic and valid, visitors will have difficulties with the site, and its accessibility will be restricted.

- the most important visitors to any site, the ones that no site can afford to exclude, are the search engines such as Google – and search engines, in effect, are blind!

You want your new site to reach as many people as possible – whoever and wherever they are and via whatever device they're using – so it must be as accessible as possible (see Box 5.4).

Usability

Usability is all about developing a site that your current and potential online customers will find easy to use. Looking at websites is now a routine part of most people's lives and they have come to expect visitor-friendly sites. They don't like surprises and every hurdle they have to overcome could represent lost business. Comfortable, convenient, coherent and conforming to expectations – these are the ingredients of a site that will keep them coming back.

What are the characteristics of a usable site? They fall into four groups:

- *presentation:* ensuring that your site's visual identity reflects the nature of your business and creates a comfortable environment; being consistent in the use of colour, typeface and layout on all pages helps visitors predict where to find what they're looking for (see Chapter 3)

- *content:* keeping the text short, clear and simple; using headings to make the text easy to scan; placing important text on the left and centre of a page; ensuring that the right information is delivered at the right stages as a visitor moves through a site – these measures all contribute to usability (see Chapter 4)

- *navigation:* making a site easy to navigate by the judicious use of text links, iconic links, free search and a site map, as described earlier in this chapter (this is arguably the most important usability characteristic)

- *feedback:* giving visitors the opportunity to provide feedback greatly enhances a site's usability; providing complete 'contact us' information (the more choice the better – people's preferred means of communication varies) and short, carefully compiled forms wherever appropriate (forms are an integral part of successful e-commerce sites; see Chapter 4)

Before a site goes online, test its usability. Ask some friends or colleagues to explore the site, and then ask them: Did you enjoy using the site? Do you understand its main purpose? Would you return to it?

BOX 5.5 The benefits of accessibility and usability

A site that adheres to the W3C guidelines on accessibility and usability is likely to:

- increase sales by encouraging visitors to stay on the site and interact with it (e.g., completing forms, buying products)
- increase revenue by reaching new visitors (e.g., in the UK, 8.6 million people – 14% of the total population – are registered as disabled, more than a third of them unable to use a screen, keyboard or mouse with ease)
- improve branding by achieving higher levels of customer advocacy (word-of-mouth recommendation is a powerful selling tool)
- improve organic search rankings by being more search engine-friendly (e.g., by using text equivalents and CSS)
- enhance customer satisfaction by giving them a good experience (remember that it's cheaper to retain old customers than to acquire new ones)
- reduce development costs because of the need to evaluate the site early in the development process and eliminate problems
- reduce the cost of customer support by creating a site that works properly

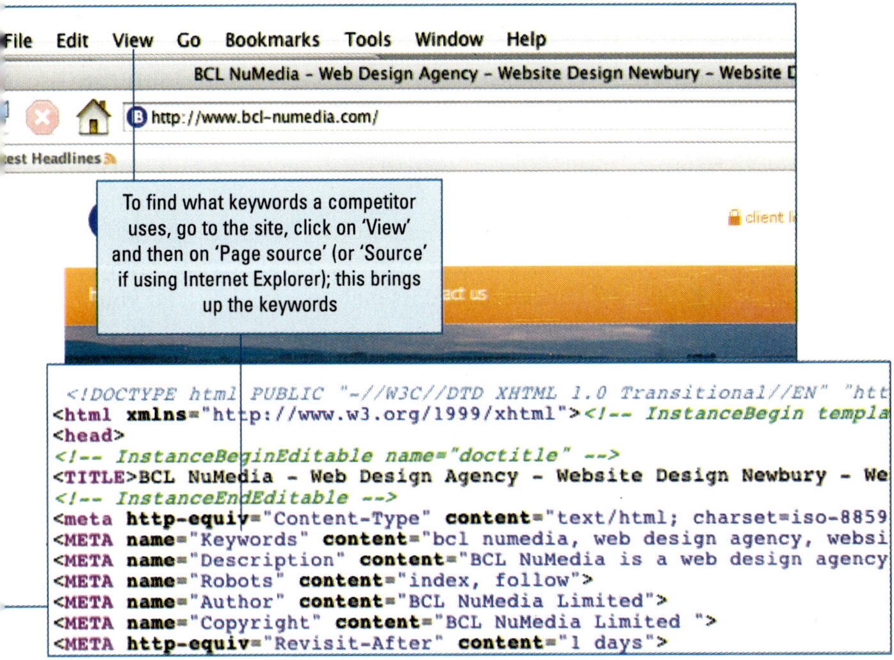

FIGURE 2.3 Checking competitors' keywords

Finding out what keywords your competitors use, especially if those competitors are highly ranked in the search engine listings, will help you decide what keywords to use to attract visitors and search engines to your site.

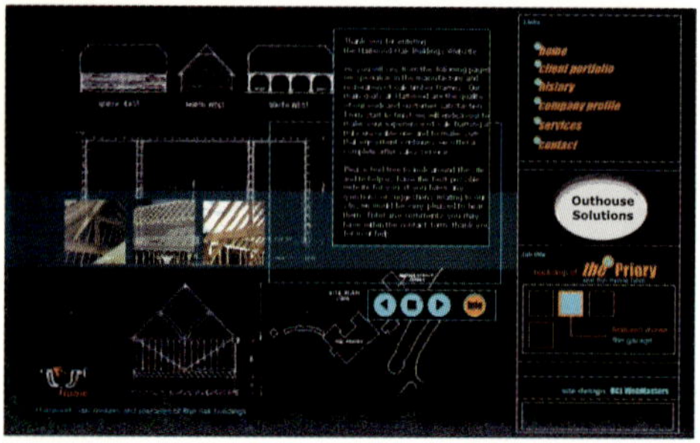

A website in 2000

- table-based
- extensive use of Flash
- crowded use of images
- fixed size
- usability problems
- distracting background music

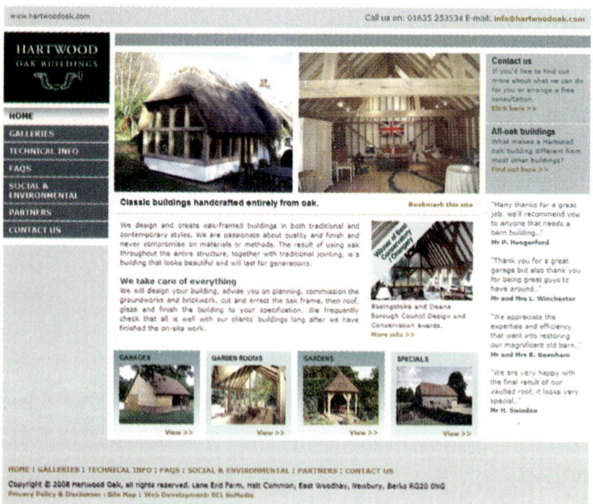

A website in 2008

- W3C compliant
- CSS / XHTML-based
- clear and informative
- fluid size, to suit a range of screen sizes

FIGURE 3.2 Website presentation, past and present

With the adoption of Cascading Style Sheets (CSS) to handle all the presentation elements of a website page (e.g., layout, typeface, colour), website development moved away from the crowded pages common at the turn of the century towards the cleaner and more professional look that characterises good websites today.

FIGURE 3.6 Using appropriate and complementary colours

Your website category determines the colours to use. For example, bold colours are common for entertainment sites, whereas subtle colours suit corporate sites, as shown in the examples above.

FIGURE 3.8 Getting the presentation right

This website uses a standard three-column format and a range of presentation elements that make it both user- and search-engine-friendly, e.g.:

- placement of standard features
- white space and overall balance
- typeface, colour, background, size and leading
- text alignment and paragraph spacing
- colour use and complementarity
- use of images, including photos and graphics

FIGURE 7.4 The major payment gateway providers

There are about 30 major payment gateway providers. They process the credit card payments made by people who buy products on your site, transferring the funds to your internet merchant account and ensuring privacy and security. Payment gateway providers vary in terms of the volume of transactions they can handle, the fees (commission, monthly, etc.) that they charge, and the cost of integration with your online shop, so it's worth taking time when choosing a provider to ensure that the one selected is the most suitable and cost-effective for your business.

When choosing a payment gateway provider, it's also worth asking:

- What credit cards can it take?
- Can it deal with multiple currencies?
- What security and fraud prevention does it offer?
- What shopping basket facility can it integrate? Does it support only certain ones?
- How often can funds be withdrawn / transferred from the account?
- What is the minimum / maximum that can be withdrawn / transferred at any one time?

FIGURE 7.5 Providing clear and timely purchase information

It's important to give visitors all the purchase information they need and to ensure that this information is where they need to see it and as early on in the process as possible. The examples in this figure show what purchase information should be displayed before the basket page; Figure 7.7 (Chapter 7) shows the detail needed on the basket page.

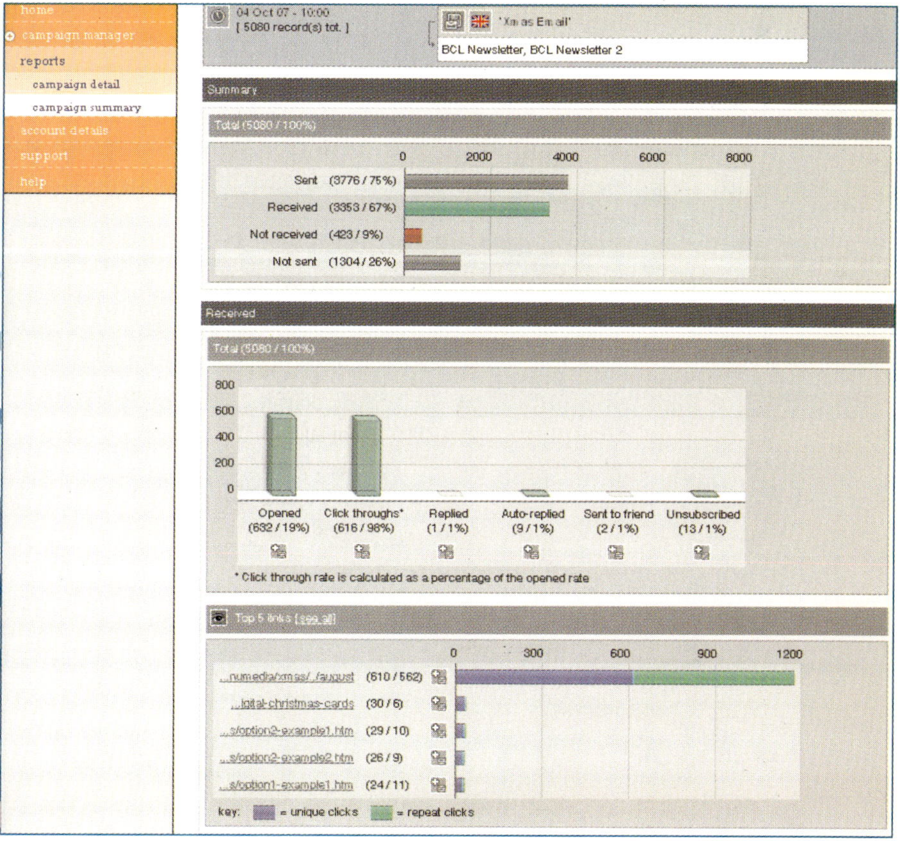

FIGURE 8.5 Measuring e-mail marketing campaign results

The level of detail in a campaign report depends on your e-mail service provider (ESP), but it should include: *open rate* (a well-targeted campaign should achieve a rate of about 30%); *click-through rate* (ideally, about 12%); *unsubscribe rate* (as low as possible); *send to a friend rate*; list of *popular links* clicked on within the e-mail; and *e-mail addresses of recipients* who clicked on links in your e-mail the most. Analyse your unsubscribers carefully; if a lot of new subscribers are dropping out it might be because you are not delivering what they expected and you need to offer more choice.

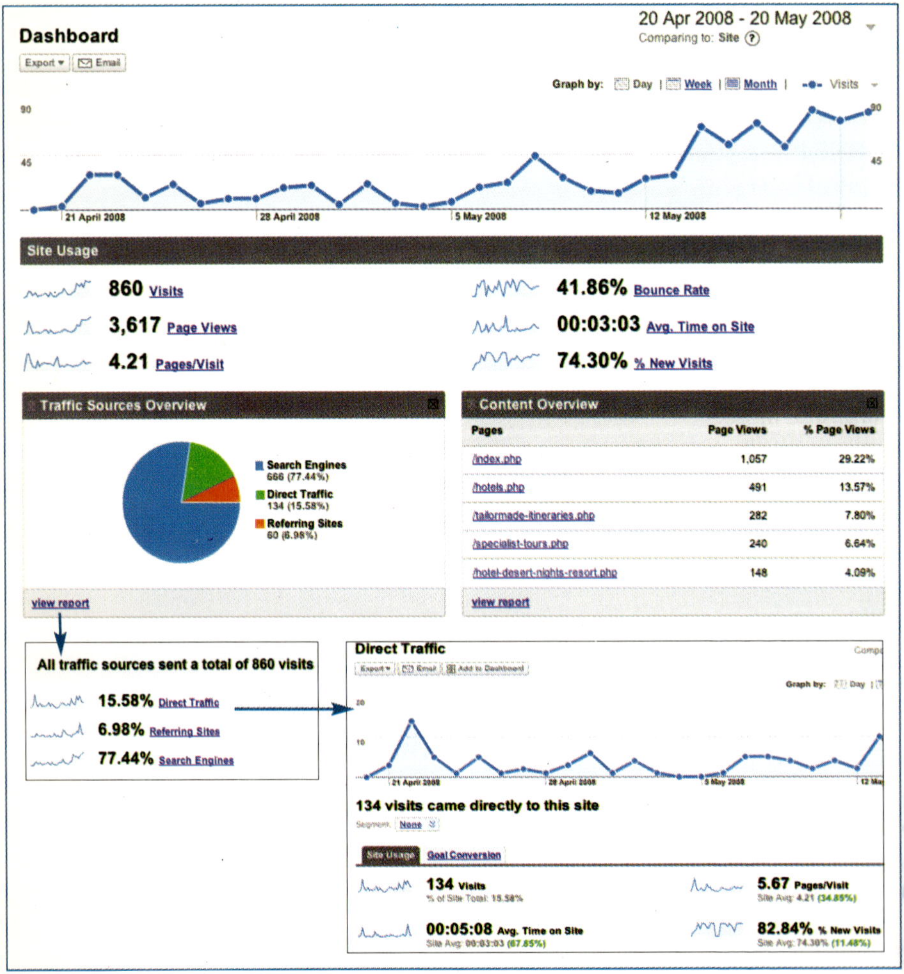

FIGURE 10.1 Analysing website performance

Using an analytics programme to assess website performance (as shown in the example here from a Google Analytics report), and then acting upon the results, is crucial to the success of a site.

Structure, presentation and behaviour

Take a look at Figure 5.3. It shows the four main components of site architecture mentioned earlier. Two of the components – structure and presentation – are on one side of the line in the 'client-side' area (visible to website visitors). The other two components – behaviour (functionality) and the databases – are on the other side the line in the 'server-side' area (a secure area, with restricted access).

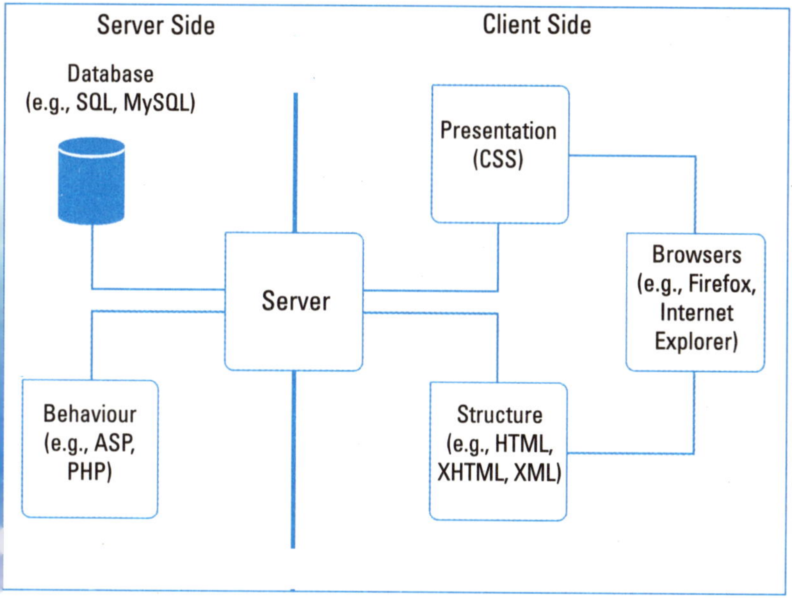

FIGURE 5.3 The four components of site architecture

Website visitors can see anything in the client-side area – the mark-up languages and the style sheets. But the server-side area is secure; only the developer, the site owner – you – and authorised people can go there, via a login.

In this context, 'client' relates to the software – such as a browser (e.g., Firefox, Internet Explorer, Opera and Safari) – that requests information from the server, interprets (decodes) it and displays it. 'Server' relates to the software – such as www servers (e.g., http) – that supplies the requested information to the 'client' software.

Structure

Most websites are written in the original language of the World Wide Web – HTML (HyperText Mark-up Language). HTML is really just a set of instructions that give website content a structure – its headings, paragraphs, lists, etc. – and create links ('hyperlinks') within this content. These instructions are read by browsers (which transfer them to the screen in a format that visitors can read) and by search engines (which 'crawl' over the content and rank the site accordingly; see Chapter 6).

There have been several versions of HTML since it first appeared in 1991, the current version (in 2008) being HTML4. But HTML has certain limitations; the mark-up language called XML (eXtensible Mark-up Language) was devised by W3C partly to overcome them. Other XML-based applications have appeared since then, the main one being XHTML (eXtensible HTML).

Presentation

As the World Wide Web grew, HTML had to take on presentation functions such as handling images, colours, typefaces, fonts and complicated layouts. This made HTML more difficult for website developers to write, and more difficult for browsers and search engines to read.

Another language was needed to take over these presentation functions. This is what CSS (Cascading Style Sheets) does. It's a style sheet language that handles content presentation and lets HTML

BOX 5.6 From tables to style sheets

Table-based websites were introduced by Netscape in the early 1990s to help developers by showing them the rows and columns of a site. Developers used these rows and columns to control page layout, although this was not the intended use. For nearly a decade, complex table-based websites were the norm, until an application created specifically to handle page layout – Cascading Style Sheets (CSS) – was introduced, allowing developers to produce more sophisticated, flexible and manageable layouts.

A major advantage of the move from tables to style sheets was that the amount of code that had to be written for page layout was significantly reduced, which accelerated page loading time and made websites easier for search engines to 'crawl'.

concentrate on content structure (see Box 5.6 and, overleaf, Figure 5.4). This has several important advantages:

- search engines are really only interested in looking at structure (HTML), so with structure separate from presentation (CSS), their search is faster and more efficient – good for SEO
- CSS enables the content to be presented in different styles (e.g., on screen, in print, by voice, in Braille and on tactile devices) – good for accessibility
- the amount of code that has to be written for presentation using CSS is far less than that using HTML, which accelerates page loading time – good for usability

Although CSS has been around since 1996, there were a lot of teething problems initially, mostly to do with browsers, and it was not until 2006 that CSS began to be widely adopted. Like the mark-up languages, its specifications are controlled by W3C.

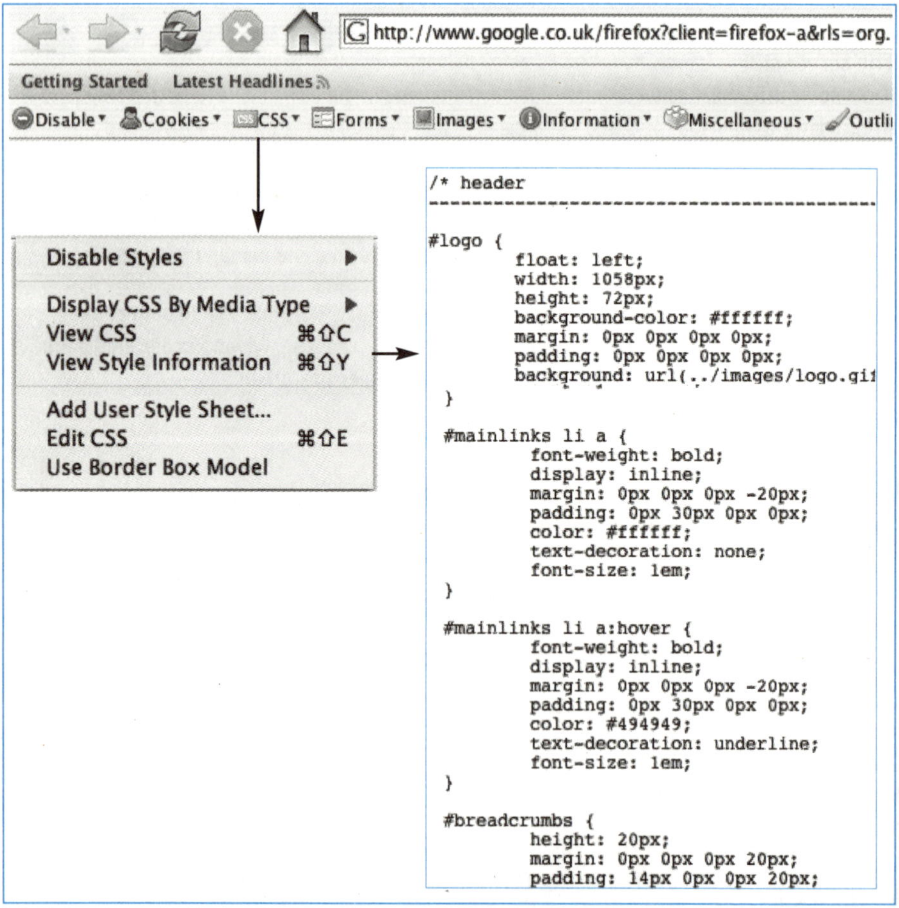

FIGURE 5.4 Specifying presentation details with CSS

Installing Web Developer (via http://chrispederick.com/work/web-developer/) gives you a useful tool bar. Via the bar's CSS icon you can see any site's CSS code, where the site's colours, layout, size, etc. are specified (if you have Internet Explorer, you can use Internet Explorer Developer instead).

Behaviour

The server-side languages provide web developers with a whole box of tools for building dynamic sites. They are what add functionality to a site, acting as a link between the visitor and the databases.

Server-side languages enable visitors, for example, to fill in forms, the content of which they then pass to the databases. When visitors sign up to receive an e-newsletter, they let the databases know. In response to a visitor's click on a button they make pop-up advertisements pop up and drop-down menus drop down. And the whole process of buying a product on line, from viewing it, getting more details, putting it in the shopping basket and following the checkout procedure, is enabled by the server-side languages, working between the visitor and the databases.

Examples of server-side languages are ASP (Active Server Pages), PHP (Hypertext Preprocessor), JSP (Java Server Pages), Perl, Python and Ruby. They work in different ways and combinations with different types of databases.

Databases

The databases on a website are the information storage areas. They are managed by database languages, such as SQL (Structured Query Language), which was developed by IBM (and originally called 'Sequel'). Most databases use SQL to handle data and many databases use it as part of a name (e.g., MS SQL, PostgreSQL and SQLite).

A database language allows developers and site administrators to retrieve, query, insert, update and delete data from the databases, and perform general management and administrative functions (see Chapter 9). A combination of SQL and one of the server-side languages enables you to computerise many basic services that you might previously have done manually (e.g., confirm orders, pass orders on to distributors, and send out invoices and statements).

Browsers, displays and search engines

There are a hundred and one things that web developers have to consider when they're building the information architecture of a site. So far, this chapter has covered the major ones. Now it's time to mention some of the others – all of them crucial if your site is to bring in more revenue.

Browsers

The purpose of a browser is to read websites. Visitors look at your website via a browser. There are many versions of browsers that they could choose from, all varying in behaviour and the degree to which they comply with W3C standards. Firefox, Internet Explorer, Mosaic and Opera, for example, are among the major browsers, but it's important also to note that AOL, MSN and Yahoo!, though usually regarded as search engines and directories, are in fact browsers as well. Most of the recent versions of browsers are W3C compliant. (For more on browsers, see Chapter 3.)

A good web development agency will ensure that your site is built so as to be compatible with the major browsers. You'll notice sometimes when you go to a site that chunks of text on the site are misplaced. This is because the site doesn't support all the browsers currently in use. The only way to be certain your site is compatible with as many browsers as possible is to test it before it goes live, so do make sure this is done.

Displays

Developers need to take account of two important display factors – resolution and colour:

- the display resolution of most screens was, until a few years ago, 800 x 600 pixels; most screens today use a resolution of 1024 x 768 pixels, and the trend is moving towards 1440 x 900 pixels (widescreen) (see Figure 5.5)

- handheld and very old computers usually use 8 bits colour hardware, giving a maximum of 256 colours; laptops and more recent computers use 16 bits hardware, giving 65,536 colours; today's computers use 24 or 32 bits hardware and can display more than 16 million colours

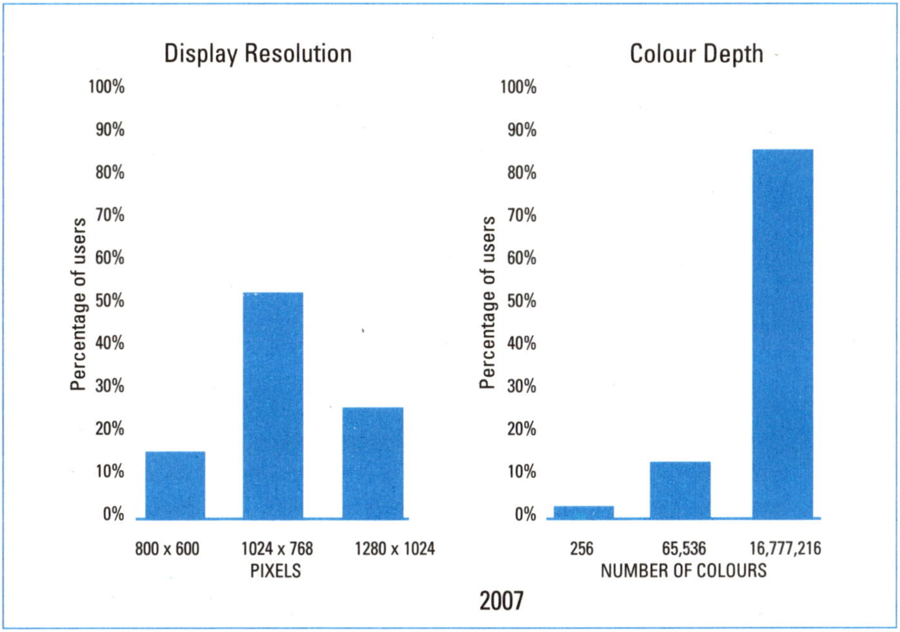

FIGURE 5.5 Display resolutions and colour depth

When developers are building a site, they need to take account of the display resolution and colour depth that most of that site's intended users are likely to have. As these graphs show, a substantial proportion of users still have 800 x 600 screens. Note that resolutions now go up to 1440 x 900 pixels.

Source: www.e-consultancy.com

When building a site, a developer must cater for the site's intended visitors in terms of screen resolution and colour. Are the visitors likely to have the latest software and relatively new computers (e.g., people in developed countries looking at garden furniture websites)? Or are they likely to have access only to old computers and software (e.g., people in developing countries looking at travel websites)?

Search engines

Chapter 6 looks at search engines in detail and at how to optimise your site, but it's worth listing here some important questions to ask while the site is being built:

- Is every page on the site accessible using text links?
- Do all the pages have a clear hierarchy of information, via headings?
- Have all the navigation systems been used, especially text links?
- Are all the images accompanied, where appropriate, by text equivalents (alt attributes)?
- If fancy graphics are used, are they used only when necessary?
- Is there a site map on every page?

In the case of sites being updated, you also need to ask about URL redirection (i.e., directing the URLs on the old site to new URLs so that the latter can be indexed by the search engines). This usually involves using a '301 Redirect', the most efficient and search engine-friendly way of handling redirects; in essence, it says to browsers and search engines: "This page has been moved, here is the new URL."

And what of the rest of the hundred and one things that you need to be aware of when your site is being built? Box 5.7 outlines some important ones.

BOX 5.7 Thinking about cookies, etc.

Here are some other things to discuss with the web developer when the site's being built.

- *CMS:* You will need a Content Management System (CMS) to manage and update your site once it's built, adding pages and functionality. There's more detail on this in Chapter 9, but you need to decide at this stage which CMS is best for you.
- *Cookies:* Some websites record visitors' activity (what they looked at, ordered, etc.) and then create 'cookies' (small text files) about this activity which they store on the visitors' computers, so that when those visitors return to the site they will not have to repeat information about themselves. Do you want your website to do this?
- *Documentation:* If your site is going to carry documents (e.g., reports, reference material), you need to decide where they'll appear, in what format, if they should be downloadable and/or searchable, how to use them to get information about people who access them (e.g., their e-mail addresses), and so on.
- *Hosting:* Websites are hosted by an Internet Service Provider (ISP), which links them to the internet and provides storage, back-up and bandwidth space. ISPs fall into three groups, and you need to decide which is best for you. Tier 1 includes the major ISPs (e.g., AT&T, CNLink, BT, Satyam and Pipex, all with direct connections to the internet via fibre optic cables). Tier 2 ISPs, used by most sites, buy bandwidth from Tier 1 ISPs. In Tier 3 (the so-called 'virtual' ISPs) you share website space with other sites, resulting in bandwidth fluctuations.
- *Page titles:* At the very top of a website page there should be a page title – a short description of what's on that page; in terms of usability and SEO, it's hard to over-emphasise the importance of having pages titles on every page of your site and making sure that they are concise, informative and compelling, are about 30–60 characters long (including spaces) and contain your site keywords (see Figure 6.2, Chapter 6).
- *Printing:* It's good idea to have a 'Print text only' facility on a site, so that users can choose to print material from your site with or without images; if you're using CSS this is easily incorporated into your site, with the printout automatically excluding images.

Chapter 6

OPTIMISATION

LET'S START WITH a few statistics:

- half the world's population now has access to the internet (that's more than 3 billion people)
- more than 90% of these people find websites via the search engines
- by 2008 there were more than 26 billion web pages for the search engines to look at
- more than 50% of online sales are driven by the search engines

Search engine optimisation (SEO) is all about building and managing a site in such a way that, when someone enters search words that are relevant to your business, your site will appear at or near the top of the organic listings on the search engine results pages (SERPS). In view of the statistics, that's a tall order!

This short chapter on optimisation is intended to highlight the most important aspects of SEO. The subject crops up throughout the book, of course, because it's so fundamental to so many aspects of website development, but at the risk of some overlap it seemed appropriate to put all the essential points about SEO here, in one place.

What is a search engine?

The names of the major search engines, accounting for about 94% of all web traffic (in 2008), will be familiar to you: Google, Yahoo!, MSN and Ask. Google is the youngest (founded in 1998) and currently the most widely used (see Figure 2.2).

A search engine uses automated 'crawlers' (also called 'bots' or 'spiders') to follow links into a website and read the pages on that site, going from page to page via the links between the pages. It then stores the pages in a giant database, where the page content is indexed and

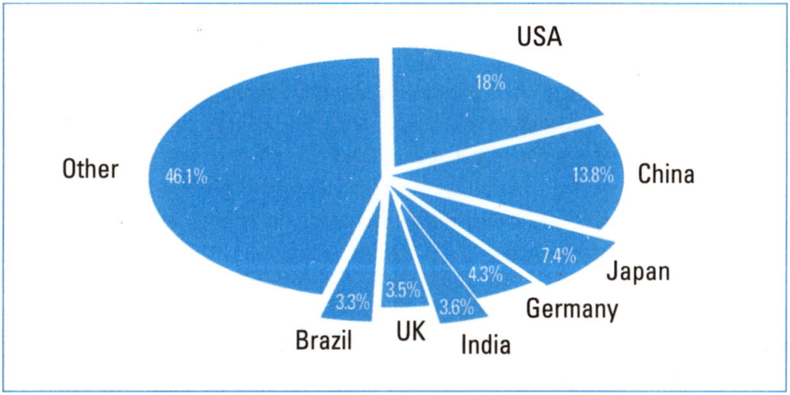

FIGURE 6.1 Share of internet users worldwide

By 2008, half the world's population had access to the internet (i.e., more than 3 billion people) and more than 90% of internet users found websites via the major search engines.

Source: www.internetworldstats.com

ranked. When the search engine receives a search query, it consults its database to find matching text and gives the enquirer a list of sites to look at, starting with those sites that it considers are:

- the most *accessible*
- the most *relevant*
- the most *popular*

What is SEO?

SEO comes under the broader concept of search engine-based marketing (SEM). SEO is one of the tools – arguably the most important one – that SEM uses to attract visitors to your site (see Chapter 8).

BOX 6.1 Using an SEO agency

It's fairly common for companies to get a site built by a web developer and then go to an SEO agency for site optimisation. If you're thinking of doing this, do take care over the agency you choose. Check to see where the agency itself is in the search engine listings if you enter a relevant phrase (e.g., 'search engine optimisation'). Ask for the URLs of sites the agency has optimised and check where these sites are in the listings. Ask about the agency's adherence to W3C standards.

As in any business, there are a few cowboys out there. They tend to charge high fees and make wild claims about getting you to the top of the listings. If they make SEO sound mysterious and complex, and seem reluctant to tell to you about the SEO techniques they use, go to another agency. There are lots of ethical agencies around who will do a good job and give you value for money.

The purpose of SEO is to get as much web traffic to your site as possible via the search engines. Optimising your site for the search engines involves:

- building *site architecture* that is easily *accessible* to search engines
- compiling *site content* that is *relevant* and attracts search engines
- obtaining *incoming links* that show search engines that your site is *popular*

Optimising the architecture

Search engines like to be able to go through a website with ease, ranking it according to a list of more than 100,000 attributes. If they encounter snags, they'll give the site a low ranking. Common snags (which go by such names as 'speed bumps' and 'walls') include: no HTML site map, poor or broken internal links, a hierarchical structure that's too deep (too many clicks to get to a desired point),

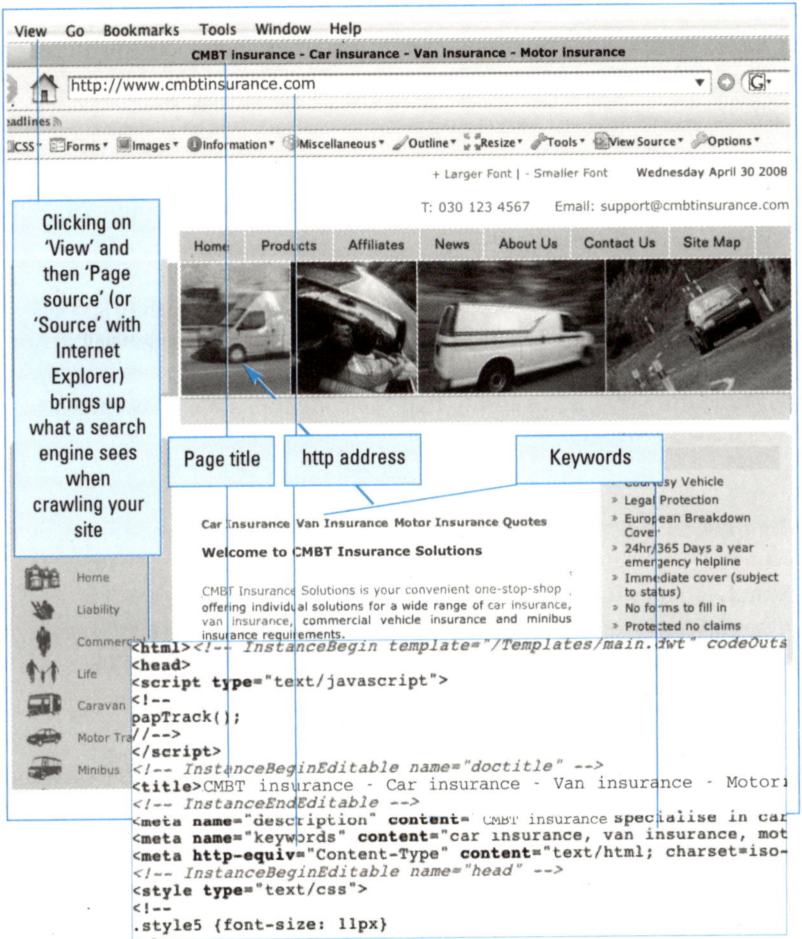

FIGURE 6.2 What a search engine sees

Fundamental to building a site with maximum optimisation is being aware of what the search engines see (e.g., words) and what they ignore (e.g., photos).

and forms that don't function properly or are too long. It's also not good to have too many drop-down menus or too many areas with restricted access (requiring login details, which search engines don't have).

The best way to ensure that search engines can crawl easily through your site is to follow the guidelines set out in Chapter 5, noting in particular the importance of:

- making the site accessible to as many browsers as possible
- using CSS so that search engines don't have to read code they're not interested in
- validating the site to ensure that the code they do read is efficient and well written

Optimising the content

Search engines rely on keywords to respond to search queries. Choosing keywords that are relevant to your site and putting them where search engines will find them easily is therefore crucial to SEO. This involves:

- compiling a list of keywords that best describe your business (see Chapter 4)
- conducting an analysis to identify which keywords to use (see Figure 6.3)
- selecting enough keywords to place two or three on each page
- embedding selected keywords in headings and prominent text (e.g., beginning of the first paragraph on a page)
- including selected keywords in the title tags (displayed on search engine listings), page titles (displayed at the top of each website page) and alt attributes (descriptions of items, such as images, that can't be rendered in text)

Report on Keyword Popularity

Position	Phrase	Daily World Searches	Competitors	KEI
1	website design	130,591	83600000	0.002
2	web design	25,681	208000000	1.234
3	website webpage design	15,304	7260000	0.002
4	webmasters	4,748	82400000	5.762
5	website designers	3,012	5730000	5.256
6	web site designers	1,172	181000000	6.475
7	website design berkshire	586	213000	0.002
8	custom website designers	513	8810000	5.822
9	web design agency	257	10900000	2.357
10	accessible web design	153	20100000	7.612
11	web design companies	< 10	0	< 0.001
12	web design newbury	< 10	0	< 0.001
13	design agency reading	< 10	0	< 0.001
14	website design reading	< 10	0	< 0.001
15	web design reading	< 10	0	< 0.001
16	web site designers berkshire	< 10	0	< 0.001
17	web site designers reading	< 10	0	< 0.001

FIGURE 6.3 Conducting a keyword analysis

Several sites provide keyword analyses (e.g., https://adwords.google.com/select/KeywordTool). They ask you to submit keywords and then they produce a report, like the one above (in this case, conducted by a Berkshire-based web design company).

Daily World Searches = the number of times a keyword is searched for daily, worldwide

Competitors = the number of other sites using this keyword

KEI = keyword effectiveness index, calculated by dividing number of searches by number of competitors; the higher the KEI, the better (i.e., many searches, few competitors)

BOX 6.2 What search engines don't like

Search engines don't like sites that are poorly coded, difficult to read or use dubious SEO tactics. They'll give them a low ranking or, at worst, remove them from their databases. So make sure your site doesn't have:

- pages stuffed with keywords
- irrelevant keywords deliberately inserted to try to attract more visitors
- hidden text (text that a user can't see, but a search engine can; e.g., white text on a white background, or text placed off the visible page)
- pages linked to each other again and again to make the site seem popular
- great chunks of text copied from high-ranking competitor sites
- an abundance of images and animation
- table-based architecture (more difficult to crawl through than a CSS-based site)
- too many pages with restricted access (search engines can't look at these pages)

As you saw in Chapter 4, there are many other aspects of site content that will make it more attractive to search engines. These include:

- creating a content-rich site (i.e., good-quality content on each page, and as many pages as possible, without overdoing it)
- keeping the page text short and coherent, with clear headings
- ensuring that all images have alt attributes – search engines can't read images
- keeping the content fresh (e.g., adding new pages, updating old pages, creating forums)

Building incoming links

Search engines set great store by the number and quality of incoming links that your site has. Often, that's the way they find your site in the first instance – picking up a link, noting that it's from a high-ranking site and following it through to your site. The more high-ranking incoming links your site has, the more popular you will appear to the search engines and the higher they will rank your site, thus attracting more traffic to it.

How do you go about getting these links? Often, a web development agency will expect you, the client, to do this on your own. First, make sure that your site has been submitted to the directories (see overleaf); acceptance by the directories will give it incoming links immediately. Then:

- check how many links are coming into your site using the method described in Figure 2.4 in Chapter 2 (enter 'links://' then a space and then your site's domain name in the search box)

- go to the site of a well-established competitor and, using the method in Figure 2.4, enter the competitor's domain name to see how many incoming links it has; do this again for your other main competitors

BOX 6.3 Useful tools for SEO tasks

There are some useful tools that help with SEO tasks, including:

Tools	*SEO tasks*
Google Tools	Keyword analysis, AdWords, Webmaster Tools
Yahoo! Search Marketing	Keyword suggestions and analysis
Web CEO	Keyword analysis, SEO submission, tracking SEO performance, building partnership links, getting ranking reports
Web Position Gold	Keyword analysis, SEO submission, tracking SEO performance, getting ranking reports
Wordtracker	Keyword analysis

- find the e-mail addresses of businesses that complement yours (preferably those with a higher ranking than your site) and of well-established sites linking to them, and send e-mails asking if they would like to link to your site (you can also use this process to set up affiliate links, described in Chapter 8)

The aim is to build permanent, relevant incoming links that will drive traffic to your site. It's an ongoing task, but an essential one if you want to retain a high ranking on the search engine listings.

Submitting sites to search engines and directories

I had client who called to say: "You've built my site, done all the SEO work – you said – but it's not there! It's not in the listings!" I replied: "There's a good reason for that. The search engines don't know about you yet."

We had only just finished building the site and were in the process of submitting it to the search engines and directories. Until that was done, and until the site's incoming links started attracting search engines, the

BOX 6.4 Checking for broken links

Broken links can occur when a website has been restructured or the ISP has been changed. They can be a serious problem when submitting the website to search engines and directories, preventing the site from being properly indexed and thus adversely affecting site rankings. They can also drive away potential customers.

It's worth going to www.google.com/webmasters/tools/siteoverview or to www.searchengineoptimising.com/link_checker/index.php to check for broken links before submitting your site. A good web development agency should do this as a matter of course after developing or amending a site.

site didn't exist as far as the search engines were concerned. No one had told them about it.

'Submitting' a site to a search engine is like saying to the search engine: "Come and look at me." It involves going to the search engine (e.g., www.google.com/addurl) and completing a form (which will include writing a short description of your site). Your site can be submitted in bulk to several search engines at one go, but it's far better to submit it to each search engine in turn.

'Submitting' a site to a web directory is also best done individually for each directory. A web directory lists websites by category, based on the subject of the website (not its individual pages, unlike search engines). Submitting a site to a directory involves going to the directory site, completing the form and choosing the directory category that best suits your site. Being on a web directory adds greatly to your link popularity.

There are hundreds of web directories to choose from (see Box 6.5 for the top 10), but note that directories will accept your site only if they

BOX 6.5 The top 10 directories

Your site should be submitted to the main directories. Currently, the top 10 are:

Ansearch	www.ansearch.com.au
Best of the Web	http//.botw.org
Business.com	www.business.com
dmoz Open Directory Project	www.dmoz.com
Google Directory	www.google.com/dirhp
JoeAnt	www.joeant.com
Starting Point	www.stpt.com
The WWW Virtual Library	http://vlib.org/
VFunk	www.vfunk.com
Yahoo! Directory	http://dir.yahoo.com

think it's good enough. The more directories that include your site, the better your page ranking will be. Some directories are free (e.g., dmoz, the largest directory on the web); some will charge for your site to be included (e.g., Yahoo! Search Directory). Don't overlook dmoz. It has categories for everything imaginable, is edited by a vast global community of editors and feeds many other web directories.

Chapter 7
E-COMMERCE

IN 2006 ONLINE RETAIL SALES in the UK reached £30 billion. In 2007 the figure was £42 billion. In 2010, it's predicted that about 36 million people in the UK will be shopping online and online retail sales will reach £60 billion. It's also predicted that, by 2020, online retail sales in the UK will account for 40% of *all* retail sales. To call this 'phenomenal' would be an understatement.

Is your business ready for this? Figures show that almost 70% of businesses in the UK are not. They haven't put their products online, mainly because they don't know how to.

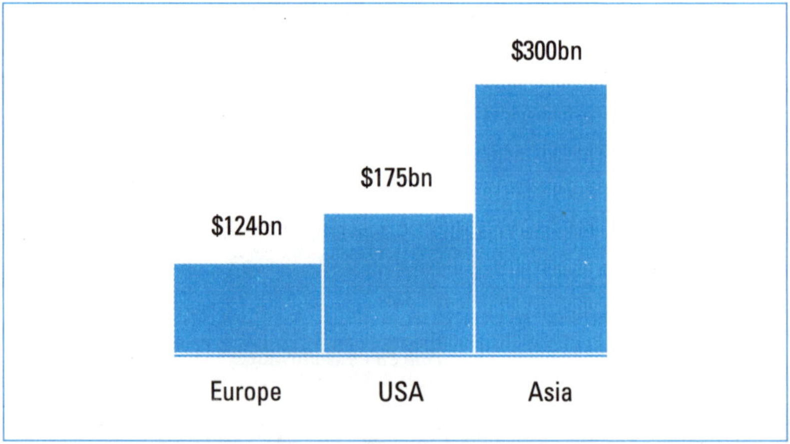

FIGURE 7.1 Volume of online sales, 2007

The volume of online sales is increasing rapidly. But these sales have been made by only about 30% of businesses, who have seen the potential of online sales and have integrated an e-commerce component into their operations. With about 85% of the world's internet users now buying online – even if it's only one product a year – it's time for all businesses to make online selling a major component of their operations.

Source: eMarketer, Forrester, IAB, Nielsen

And it's the same story in much of the developed world, including the rest of Europe, the USA and the emerging economies in Asia and South America. The roughly 30% of businesses worldwide that have understood and integrated an e-commerce component into their operations are sitting pretty. The rest have a lot of catching up to do, and they need to do it now or risk falling by the wayside.

What does 'e-commerce' mean? It's the buying and selling of products (commerce) via electronic (e-) means. Or, more simply, it's trading online. There are two types of e-commerce: business-to-business (B2B) and business-to-consumer (B2C). This chapter looks at both types and how they determine what e-commerce package is best. Then it looks at three elements you need to get right when building your online shop:

- choosing the payment gateway provider
- having a clear sales proposition
- ensuring that the checkout process is simple, fast, focused and reassuring

BOX 7.1 The top 10 players globally in online sales

Currently, the top 10 players in online sales worldwide are:

1. Google sites
2. Microsoft sites
3. Yahoo! sites
4. Time Warner Network
5. eBay
6. Wikipedia sites
7. Amazon sites
8. Fox Interactive Media
9. Apple Inc.
10. CNET Networks

All the work that has been outlined up to this point – setting your objectives, researching your competitors and customers, and creating a site with a great visual identity and well-written and search-engine-friendly content and architecture – will have been worthwhile if you get these three elements right. Get them wrong, though, and your potential customers will leave your site before they've completed the checkout process, whether or not it's a great site in all other respects.

Business-to-business

In traditional (offline) business, trading with end-users was known as 'consumer marketing' and trading with other businesses was known as 'industrial marketing'. With the advent of e-commerce in the mid-1990s, these terms were replaced by B2B and B2C, respectively.

Setting up B2B facilities means using an e-commerce package that includes:

- a range of administrative functions (finance, invoicing, stocktaking, deliveries, etc.) to streamline the business
- customer-specific accounts that hold information on each customer (contact details, stock levels, credit limit, payment history, etc.) and are accessible to both the business and the customer

B2B e-commerce packages are changing the way that people do business with each other (see Figure 7.2). Your distributor is low on stock and needs to re-order from you? It'll take him a few seconds to do it online; no need to talk to anyone or wait for pieces of paper confirming the order. He needs to track a delivery? Done online in a few seconds. He's not sure when his next payment to you is

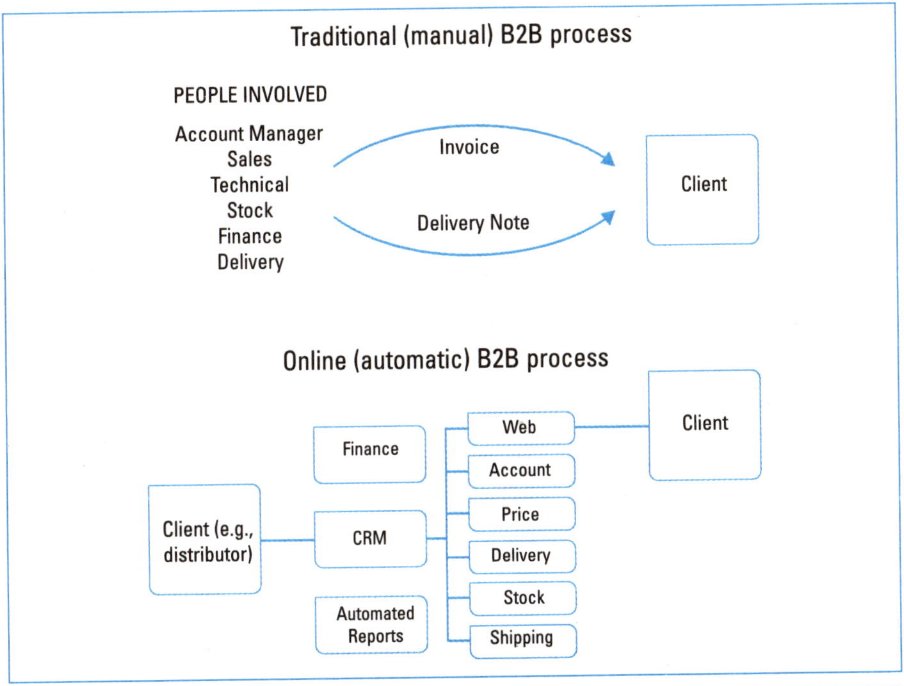

FIGURE 7.2 Traditional and online B2B processes

In the traditional B2B process, a client (e.g., your distributor) places an order via the Account Manager. The message is relayed through the Sales, Technical, Stock, Finance and Delivery sections; an invoice and a delivery note are raised. All this involves phone calls, form filling, and time.

In the online B2B process, a client who wants to place an order goes to your site, accesses his client account (holding his contact details, payment history, credit limit, etc.), links to the relevant product page (with information on price, delivery, stock, etc.), orders the product and then tracks its delivery. Everything he does is fed to the Customer Relationship Management (CRM) area, with his client account information being updated (Finance) and reports being produced, all automatically.

due? His online account will not only tell him what's due and when, but will also enable him to make the payment in seconds. Invoicing and being invoiced, in the traditional sense, are becoming a thing of the past in the B2B world.

There are many e-commerce packages available (see Box 7.2).

BOX 7.2 Useful e-commerce packages

There are many e-commerce packages available for B2B and B2C use for small to medium-sized businesses. Some software companies will host and license packages, others do either one or the other. If you use licensed software, that means you can host it wherever you want, with no restrictions.

Leading e-commerce software companies include:

Company	*Hosted*	*Licensed*
Actinic	Yes	Yes
CommerceNow	Yes	Yes
EKM Sytems	Yes	No
Epages	Yes	Yes
Hybris	No	Yes
Magicalia	Yes	No
Maginus	Yes	Yes
Moneyspyder	Yes	No
Shopcreator	Yes	Yes
Truiton	Yes	No
Venda	Yes	No

Companies that provide enterprise-level e-commerce packages (for large businesses) include ATG, e-InBusiness, Lavasuite, Snow Valley and Summit Media.

Business-to-consumer

The B2C e-commerce world is all about direct online selling and buying between retailers (including distributors and manufacturers) and customers. You (the retailer) have a product to sell, you want to sell it online, you've done all your homework on customers and competitors, and you've lined up a web development agency to build your site. Now you need to decide what e-commerce package is most likely to encourage people to buy your products online.

You have three options:

- a licensed package
- a managed / hosted package
- a bespoke application

What is your budget?

Licensed B2C e-commerce packages can cost anything from £100 upwards. Among the most common ones is Actinic, widely used among SMEs (see Box 7.2). It has all the basics you need in an e-commerce package: cross selling, e-mail services, invoicing, product search engine, promotions, metadata management, reporting, and delivery calculations.

A managed / hosted solution involves paying a monthly fee (about £20) to an e-commerce software company. Again, the process is simple, but it needs a bit more computer literacy than installing licensed packages. You lease space and software from the software company and you use the software to create a design, upload words (product descriptions) and images (of products), and add the checkout and payment facilities. If you choose this route, do check that the software uses CSS, to make life easy for the search engines. The downside of a managed solution is that you don't own your online shop, only its contents, so you can't

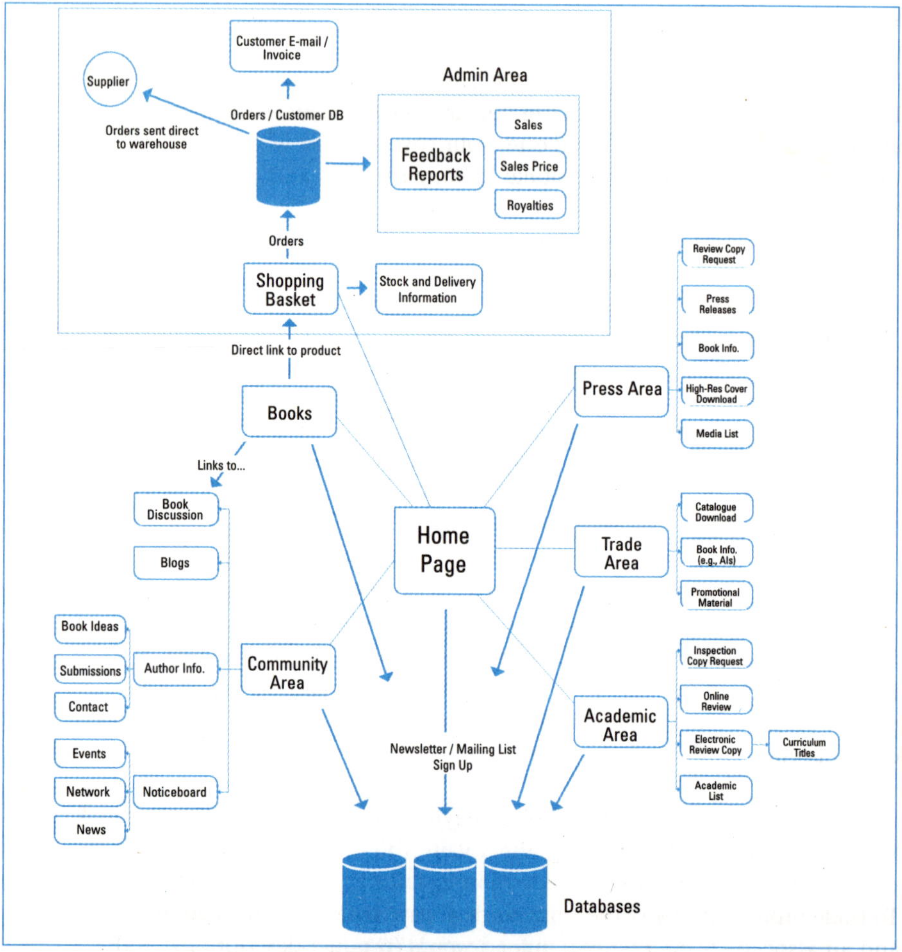

FIGURE 7.3 A model for an e-commerce site

This model was created for a book publisher's e-commerce website. The e-commerce area of the model is in the boxed area, top left.

sell it to anyone. Also, the design of managed solutions often looks unprofessional.

For a bespoke B2C e-commerce site you go to a web development agency. Take care to find a good one. Your costs could run into the thousands if you want a professional looking site. Ask the questions that need to be asked:

- Do the agency adhere to W3C standards?
- Do they have their own e-commerce software? (Often, this will be modified existing software)
- Will they give you a demonstration of the e-commerce software they use?
- Will they give you the URLs of other e-commerce sites they've built?
- What experience do they have with sites that started small and grew big?
- Does their software support APIs? (An application programming interface, which enables different programs to 'talk' to each other) If not, this will create problems later in integrating internal applications.

Remember, you're looking for a web development agency that has proven programming experience with e-commerce sites, not a graphic design agency that will make your site look pretty.

Payment gateway providers

To trade online you need the services of a 'payment gateway provider' and an associated 'internet merchant account' (IMA) from an acquiring bank, which give websites the means to take credit card payments securely. New companies, or those with a poor credit track record, sometimes have difficulties getting an IMA. All payment gateway providers charge a flat monthly rate or a transaction fee (usually a percentage of what the customer pays for your product), as well as a fee for integrating their system with your online shop. Some payment gateway providers charge additional fees to cover such things as extra security. The major payment gateway providers are shown in Figure 7.4 (colour page V).

If you're using a web development agency, it should have worked with several of the major payment gateway providers and be able to advise on the most suitable one for you (see Box 7.3). I generally know exactly which payment gateway provider to choose for a client when I have the answer to these questions: "What is your average cost of sale?" and "What is your expected volume?"

BOX 7.3 Finding a suitable payment gateway provider

One of my clients started up in 2004 as a small online business selling handpainted scarves. Their growth over the following 4 years was so phenomenal it took everyone by surprise. This meant, among other things, that they had outgrown their original payment gateway provider and needed to move to one that had lower commission charges and enhanced security features. In choosing new providers for them, we also had to cater for the substantial proportion of their sales now coming from the USA; this meant including PayPal, one of the biggest providers in the USA.

The sales proposition

Think of a website as a department store. There's an area in the store that sells stationery. You want to buy some stationery. When you entered the store (1), the décor, layout and general ambience made you feel comfortable and told you that you'd probably find what you were looking for. Now you're in the stationery area (2), which you found easily. You note that it's well stocked and easy to browse, with the products well displayed and clearly priced. There's a payment desk that looks as you'd expect it to look, and you know it'll take just a minute or two to pay for your purchase at the desk (3) before leaving the shop, your transaction complete.

In website terms, (1) is the home page, (2) is the product page and (3) is the shopping basket page. Just as a department store tells you in a variety of ways what its sales proposition is (product location, quality, range, price, purchasing procedure, etc.), so a website must make it sales proposition clear to visitors throughout their visit.

A website sales proposition should consist of:

- product details (e.g., image, description, function, availability)
- price details (e.g., cost with / without sales tax, special offers, bulk discounts, gift options)
- payment details (e.g., guarantees, privacy, security, payment options)
- delivery details (e.g., options, carriers, charges, times, conditions)
- registration details – if required, and if so what the benefits are (see Box 7.4)

BOX 7.4 Customer registration

It's tempting to let customers buy products from your online shop without registering, for fear they'll feel hassled by having to register while buying the products. But there are benefits for customers if they do register (e.g., not having to re-enter personal details on subsequent visits; being able to track product delivery) and for you (e.g., expanding your mailing list). The registration process should be quick, easy and – above all – optional, with the benefits clearly spelled out.

The best approach is to offer optional registration near or at the end of the purchase (see Figure 7.7, page 109). By the time customers have entered their address and payment information, they will probably realise the benefits of registration and, at this stage, all they'll need to enter is a password.

You need to make all these sales proposition elements as clear as you can and as early as you can in the buying process (see Figure 7.5, colour page VI). A visitor who lands on a site, finds a product he wants to buy, puts it in the shopping basket and then moves to the checkout, only to be told at this late stage "Whoops! sorry, it's not available" or "By the way, there's a delivery charge" or "Oh dear, apologies, we don't take that particular credit card", is a visitor who will leave your site empty-handed very quickly and probably not return.

The checkout process

The term 'shopping basket abandonment' is not something you want associated with your site.

An average of about 48% of people who have already put items in the shopping basket and proceeded to checkout abandon websites before actually making the purchase. Why? Because the checkout process has not followed basic principles.

The checkout process should be:

- *simple*, guiding buyers along a logical and well-signposted route
- *fast*, with no requests for information from the customer that is not absolutely necessary
- *focused*, with the purchase the sole aim, and no distractions or broken links along the way
- *reassuring*, with guarantees on privacy and security and on product quality and delivery

Figure 7.6 lists the most common reasons for shopping basket abandonment, given in a survey. You'll see that most of the reasons transgress the basic checkout process principles.

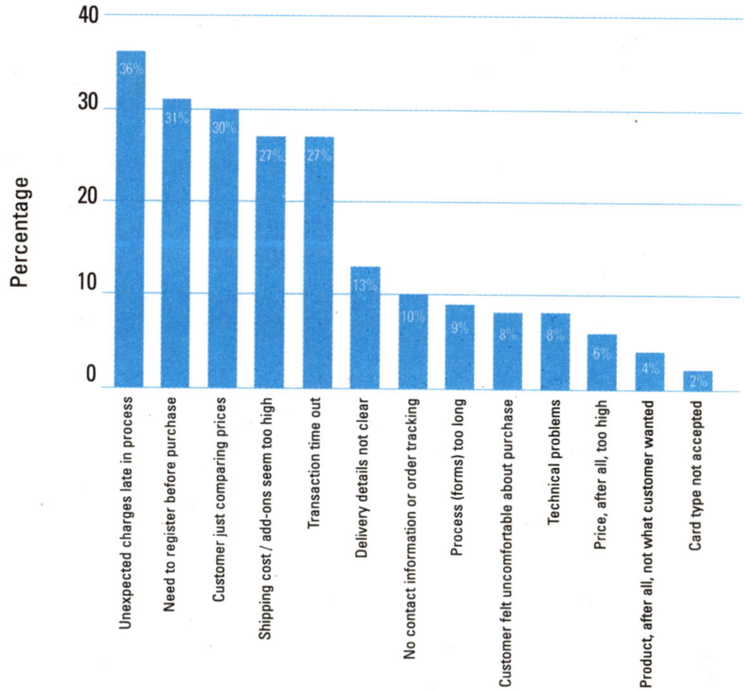

FIGURE 7.6 Reasons for 'shopping basket abandonment'

It's important to adhere strictly to the basic checkout process principles to prevent potential buyers from dropping out of the process before completing a purchase. As the figure shows, there are many reasons why potential buyers do this, but most of them are preventable.

Source: www.e-consultancy.com

A well-formulated checkout process is one that strikes a good balance between, on the one hand, the customer's needs and expectations and, on the other, what you (the online retailer) need to know and want to achieve.

The customer needs to know:

- What am I buying?
- What's the cost, including delivery?
- When will it be delivered?
- How do I pay and is it secure?
- Is the payment process quick and where am I in it?
- Has my order been successful?

You need to know:

- What the customer is buying
- The customer's name and contact details
- The customer's delivery and billing addresses
- The customer's payment details
- That the payment has been verified, so that purchase and delivery details can be confirmed

The customer expects to:

- Get through the process quickly
- Provide as little information as possible
- Leave the checkout area and return later without having to start again
- Avoid having to re-enter all details on subsequent visits to the site
- Make changes if necessary
- Get immediate purchase and delivery confirmation

You want to:

- Keep the customer online
- Get the required information from the customer
- Ensure that the customer buys the product
- Encourage the customer to come back again
- Conduct sales analyses

The purchase and checkout forms that customers complete should embody all these elements. And the order confirmation that they receive should reassure them that the transaction has been successful.

For good examples of a purchase form and an order confirmation, see Figures 7.7 and 7.8, respectively

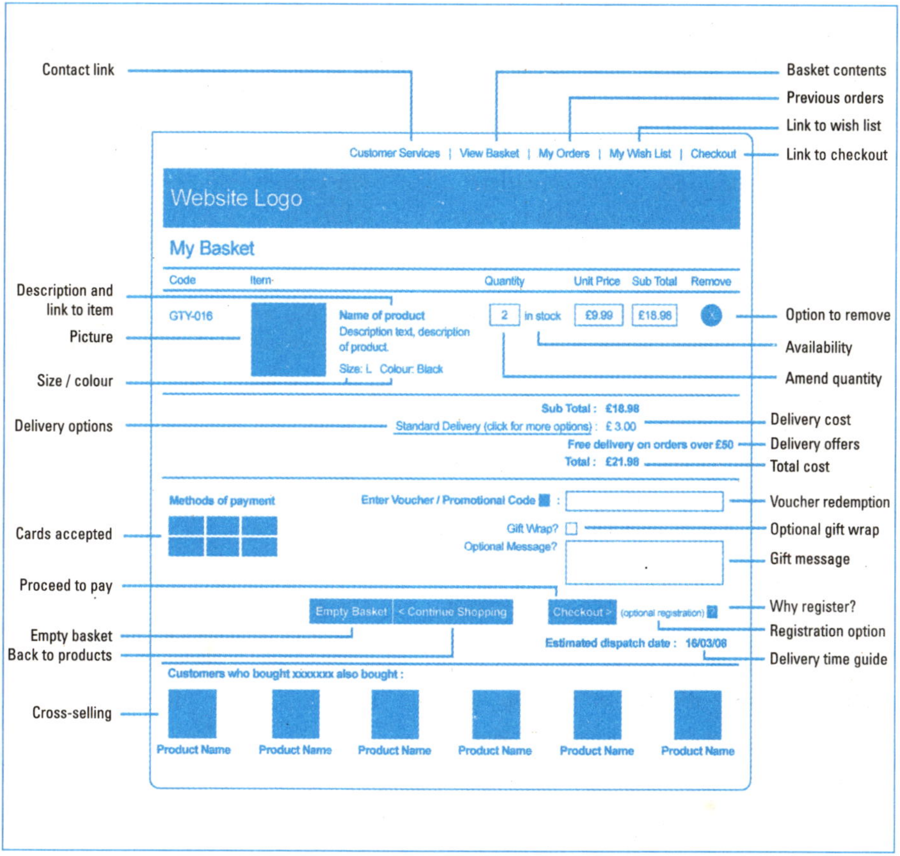

FIGURE 7.7 Purchase form information

This example of a purchase form gives an idea of the information that customers need to know when making a purchase. A customer left, at this stage of the process, with questions about such things as product availability, credit cards accepted, delivery cost and delivery date will probably 'abandon the shopping basket' and drop out.

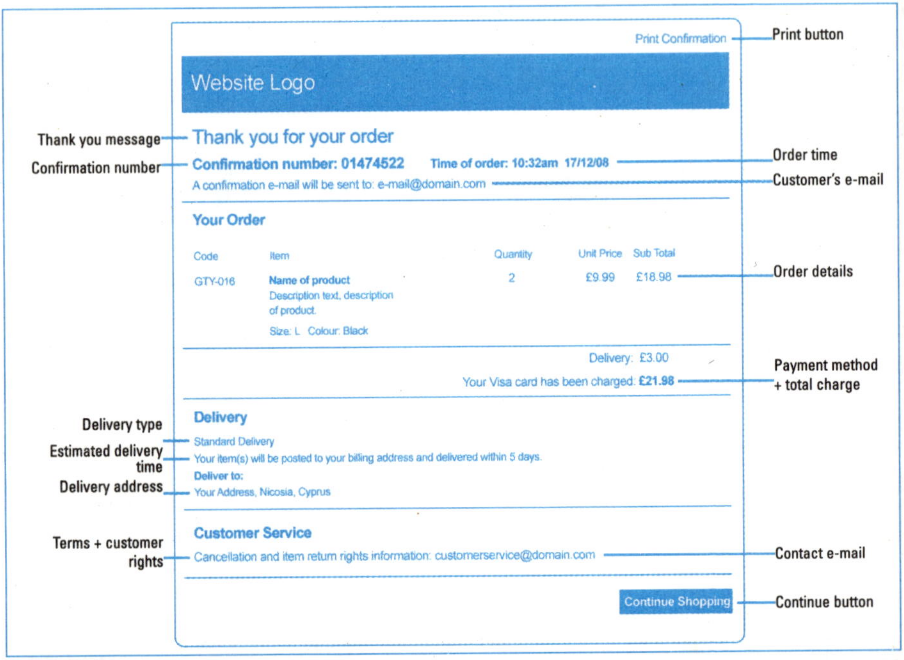

FIGURE 7.8 Order information details

A purchase order confirmation with all the details that customers need to know, as in the example here, gives customers peace of mind and will encourage them to visit the site again.

There are two fundamental ingredients of an effective e-commerce area:

- getting the big issues right (the payment gateway provider, the sales proposition and the checkout process)
- getting the detail right (the information you give and need, the purchase form design and information, and the order confirmation)

And there is one final recommendation – test, test, test, before going live.

Chapter 8

E-MARKETING

THE NET IS, ARGUABLY, the world's least expensive and most effective marketing tool. The top international companies have known this for some years. Medium-sized businesses are now discovering it too. And some of the smallest businesses, especially entirely web-based ones, were among the first to see that the return on investment (ROI) in e-marketing was significant and, because of their size, were able to exploit this new tool faster than other businesses.

But there are many businesses that aren't on board because they're confused by the techno-babble that accompanies the subject and they don't know where to start. And yet, of all the things to learn and do in order to create a profitable online business, e-marketing – for the non-technical business person – should be the easiest.

What does 'e-marketing' mean? It means using electronic means to sell your products. The basics of marketing don't change: advertising, branding, customer relations, mailing, PR, etc. It's only the media – the web and e-mail – that differ, and the ways of using them to reach and retain customers in numbers that traditional marketing methods can only dream about.

There are three categories of e-marketing:

- web-based marketing
- search-engine-based marketing (SEM)
- e-mail marketing

This chapter looks at the marketing tools in each of these categories. By the end of the chapter you should see e-marketing for what it really is – a formidable and flexible marketing approach that's easy to understand, exciting to implement and, potentially, very rewarding. You have only to look at the huge increase in expenditure on e-marketing in recent years to see that the rewards must be worth the investment (see Figure 8.1).

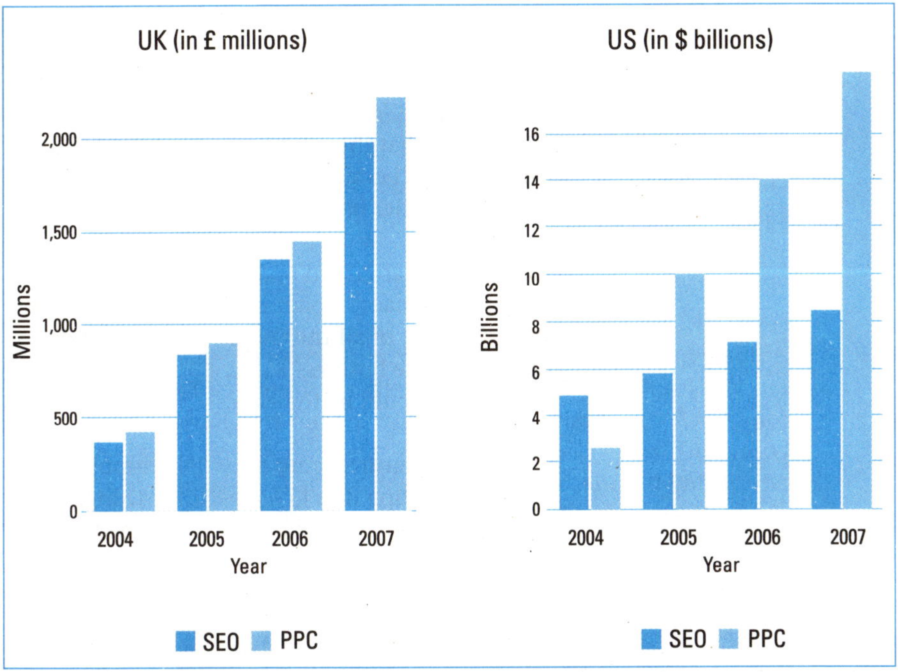

FIGURE 8.1 Expenditure on SEM in the USA and the UK, 2005–2007

The statistics for search-engine-based marketing (SEM) in the UK and the USA indicate that more and more businesses are now seeing the internet as a very effective marketing tool, with a great return on investment (ROI). Effective marketing mechanisms include search engine optimisation (SEO) and pay-per-click (PPC) campaigns.

Source: www.e-consultancy.com

Take care to invest in e-marketing wisely and incrementally. There are some e-marketing 'specialists' out there who promise the earth and charge it too. Taking on board the guidance offered in this chapter could save you a lot of money.

Web-based marketing

A website itself and many of its standard features (e.g., blogs, forums, product pages and newsfeeds), as well as how it links to the web community via affiliate marketing – all these are marketing tools that come under the umbrella of web-based marketing. The other two categories of e-marketing – SEM and e-mail – are add-ons supported by websites.

Affiliate marketing

Affiliate marketing is one of the best and cheapest e-marketing tools around. It involves being linked to other websites (affiliates) that, for a small commission, refer business to your website via a specially coded link. It has become so popular that it's redefining the way advertising is done, moving away from the 'pay-an-advertiser-and-hope-for-the-best' model towards a 'pay-for-performance-only' model.

BOX 8.1 The birth of affiliate marketing

Legend has it that affiliate marketing was born when Jeff Bezos, CEO and founder of Amazon, was chatting to a woman at a cocktail party who wanted to sell books about divorce on her website. He came up with the idea of allowing her to put a link to Amazon on her site and paying her a commission every time someone clicked on this link and bought a book from Amazon.

Understandably, many businesses are now devoting much effort to signing up as many affiliates as possible, some going into the thousands. They've seen the figures, they've looked at the results. In 2007 affiliate marketing in the UK grew by an estimated 45%, with the total value of online sales generated by affiliate marketing alone exceeding £3 billion.

There are many off-the-shelf affiliate software packages that can handle the whole procedure for you. The procedure involves:

- processing new affiliate sign-ups
- tracking all sales referred to your site by affiliates
- calculating the commission owed to affiliates
- making the commission payments automatically

With the assistance of your web development agency, affiliate packages are easy to set up and offer a lot of flexibility. They will let you, for

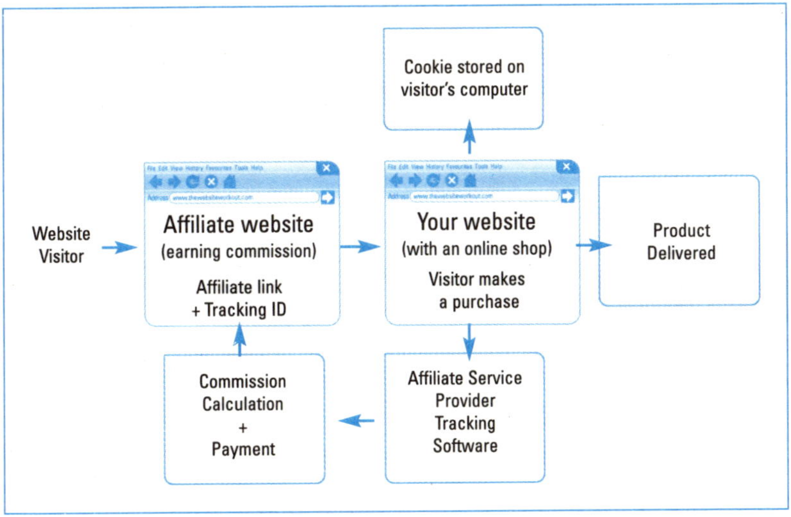

FIGURE 8.2 The affiliate marketing process

A major attraction of affiliate marketing is that, once you have put in the initial work of setting up the links, the system is fully automated and there's nothing more you need to do – apart from setting up even more links.

Source: Adapted from Davis, H. 2006. Google Advertising Tools. *O'Reilly, CA, USA*

example, vary the basis on which the commission is paid. The choice includes:

- CPM (cost per thousand impressions): you pay affiliates for every 1000 advertisements of yours that they show ('M' stands for 'thousand')

- CPC (cost per click): you pay affiliates every time a visitor to their site clicks through to yours, whether or not a sale is made

- CPS (cost per sale): you pay affiliates a fixed percentage of the sale of a product to a visitor they've referred to your site – one of the most common methods

- CPL (cost per lead): you pay affiliates for leads to the contact information of potential customers, often via a new affiliate website – particularly common in the insurance sector

A recent arrival on the affiliate marketing scene is the concept of aggregate affiliates (also known as 'power affiliates' or 'affiliate solution providers'). Instead of you contacting, individually, all the websites you know that target a similar customer base to yours and asking them to join your affiliate programme, you approach an aggregator who will have hundreds of such websites and will set up your affiliate links with them. This is well worth considering if you have a lot of products to sell.

Blogs

A blog is a personal journal put up on the net (we*b log*). Typically, it focuses on one topic and doesn't require much formatting. So it's simple to create and, because each blog has its own URL, it's an easy way of adding new URLs, which increase a site's popularity with search engines. A blog is an ideal vehicle for advertising your business and its products, and the syndication that's built into blog management (making blogs, in effect, a type of newsfeed, though few people realise

BOX 8.2 Linking to blogs

Chapter 2 showed you how to find out how many sites link to your site. But that didn't include the blogs that link to your site. You can find out how many sites *and* blogs link to you by entering in the search box: related:: www.*your domain name*.com (note the double colon and space before www).

To create a blog, go to www.blogger.com, owned by Google, or take a look at http://wordpress.com or www.typepad.com, both of which offer a lot of functionality.

this) means that the advertisement could reach a wide audience. So the blog will attract visitors to your site who wouldn't otherwise find it. That's a lot of benefits from a marketing tool that costs nothing!

If you use blogs as an e-marketing tool – and you should – do keep them up to date. Out-of-date website items are a turn-off for potential buyers.

Forums

Forums, message boards, chat rooms – these are often unsung heroes in the e-marketing world and yet they can be a great way to attract visitors who weren't looking for your site at all. I touched earlier on their role in creating a content-rich site, keeping it fresh and attracting search engines (see Chapter 4). What I want to highlight here is how they can be used to market your website and its products.

Forums are interactive areas on a site that encourage visitors to post information, express opinions, and ask and answer questions. In their writing, these visitors tend to use terms and phrases about a topic that a person seeking information about that topic might enter in a search box. That person would then, unexpectedly, land on your site – and discover an online shop he didn't know was there. Setting up and managing forums can be time-consuming, but doesn't cost much and can generate a lot of revenue.

BOX 8.3 E-marketing software

Many software applications you'll need for e-marketing are available, free, from Google Webmaster Tools. Web development agencies that have been around a while should have most of them, and over the years they will have modified them in different ways to suit different customers. So if you ask a web development agency to create a bespoke site for you, they should charge for modifying existing applications, not for the vastly more expensive (and usually unnecessary) process of creating applications from scratch. When you're discussing applications with your web development agency, it's worth asking "Do you already have something like it?"

Take a look at the Google Webmaster Tools catalogue on www.Google.com/webmasters. It's full of uploaded applications and application-related information. Apart from Google Webmaster Tools, there are many other online sources of applications, and most of them provide free application programming interface (API) packages.

Product pages

As you saw in Chapter 6, a product page is the page that carries the details of a product you're selling. It's like a marketing brochure, containing attractive images and comprehensive information on the product, but it's online and has its own URL.

Always ensure that the content of your product pages is relevant. If visitors find that these pages don't contain what the page URLs suggests they do (i.e., their content is irrelevant), they'll be annoyed and probably leave, and search engines won't give you any brownie points either. It's like producing a printed brochure with a title on the outside that doesn't relate to the text and images inside.

Newsfeeds

A newsfeed, often referred to as an RSS newsfeed, is news content published and constantly updated by a website that delivers it to you, when and how you want it, usually for a subscription fee.

You can also create newsfeeds yourself. RSS stands for 'Really Simple Syndication' and an RSS newsfeed can be a really simple e-marketing tool.

There are three types of newsfeeds you can set up on your website that will add interest, content and links, which is good for SEO:

- a newsfeed service that covers a range of subjects (e.g., finance, travel and property) and supplies your site with news related to your business
- newsfeeds from specific organisations that would be of interest to your target customers (e.g., a finance sector company could choose newsfeeds from Bloomberg, BBC, EIN and *The Financial Times*)
- a newsfeed that you create about your business, carrying at least 10 items and adding to them weekly (while archiving the replaced news items so that they can still be found by search engines)

Search-engine-based marketing (SEM)

Any form of e-marketing that aims to promote a website by increasing its ranking on the search engine results pages (SERPS) falls under the SEM umbrella. The main SEM tools are SEO and pay-per-click (PPC) campaigns. Until the advent of CSS, Google site maps were also an SEM tool (see Box 8.4).

BOX 8.4 Google site maps

A 'Google site map' should not be confused with a 'site map' (as described in Chapter 5). A Google site map is the code written into a site's architecture to make it easier for search engines to look at your site content and index your site pages. If your site is table-based, then it's important to have a Google site map. If it uses CSS, however, a Google site map is not necessary because CSS separates the content code from the presentation code, making it easier for search engines to find what they want.

Search engine optimisation

As discussed in detail in Chapter 6, SEO involves:

- making your site structure and content attractive to search engines
- building links from high-ranking sites into your site
- submitting your site to search engines and the major directories

Implemented well, all these methods will help to push your site higher up the listings, bringing it to more people's attention. And that's a major objective of any marketing campaign – making people notice you.

Pay-per-click

When you search for something on the net, your search results appear in a column in the centre of the page. On the right-hand side of the page is a narrower column. The items in this right-hand column are all, in effect, advertisements. They have appeared there in response to the words a visitor entered in the search box. How did they get there? As a result of a PPC campaign, one of the most lucrative e-marketing tools.

PPC advertising is a way of putting your site URL in front of potential customers searching for the sort of product that you're selling online. It's a great way of getting onto page 1 of the listings. Here's how it works:

- you select some keywords (about 20 phrases) that you think potential customers might enter (see Chapters 4 and 6)

- you write an advertisement with a concise title (3–4 words) and text (up to 12 words) containing the keywords, and adding your site URL

- you submit your advertisement to a so-called 'paid placement' network (e.g., Google AdWords, Yahoo! Search Marketing or Microsoft adCenter)

- someone looking at the search results notices your advertisement in the right-hand column and clicks on it

- the cost of each click (can vary from a few cents to more than £10) is deducted from the amount you've agreed to pay the network (based on cost per keyword), until that downpayment is used up (e.g., if you put up £100, with each click costing £1, your advertisement stays online till 100 people have clicked on it, and is then removed)

The advertisement should take visitors straight to the relevant page – the landing page (not the home page); the most successful campaigns are those that run many adverts linking to many landing pages.

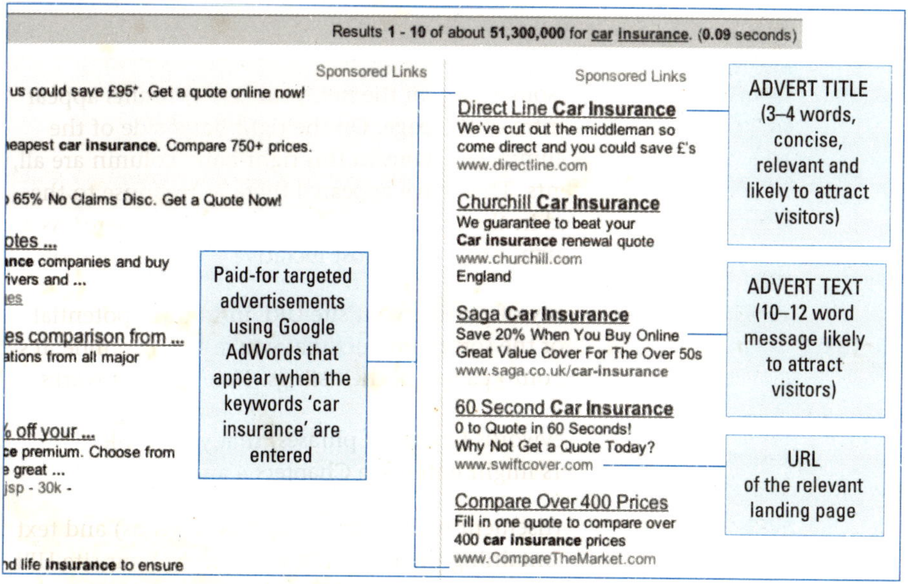

FIGURE 8.3 Targeted advertisements on the listings

The right-hand side of the search engine results pages (SERPS) is usually occupied by paid-for targeted advertisements, many of them there as part of a pay-per-click (PPC) campaign. The ranking of these paid-for advertisements depends on how much was paid per keyword.

BOX 8.5 Running a viable PPC campaign

One of our clients was spending £400 a day on a PPC campaign and was getting a good conversion rate (3%). The paid placement network that our client had used analysed what visitors were looking for and recommended that our client pay £600 to increase the conversion rate to 4%. We tested this for a week for our client, but the test showed that, proportionately, our client would be paying more for less. So they carried on as before.

The greater your payment per keyword that a visitor selects, the higher your ad will appear. You should bid on keywords with the aim of getting your ad placed in the most cost-effective position (about four or five items down from the top of the right-hand column). The more popular the keywords, the higher you are likely to have to bid.

Do remember that running a PPC campaign is a bit of a gamble, so don't spend too much on it until you're sure it's worth it (see Box 8.5). You also need to be aware that PPC campaigns can be abused – competitors might click repeatedly on your ad simply to reduce your downpayment – but search engines can detect this and will protect your investment.

E-mail marketing

E-mail marketing is one of the most cost-effective e-marketing tools. It means, simply, using e-mail to market your business and products directly to customers. An e-mail marketing campaign can be tailored to suit different groups of customers, costs a fraction of what direct mail costs, is an effective way of building e-relationships and its impact can be easily measured.

The most common e-mail marketing tools are:

- mass-marketing broadcasts (a single e-mail message sent out to as many people as possible; sometimes called 'e-shots')

- transactional e-mails (where recipients can buy your products directly from an e-mail message, without being redirected to your website)
- customer satisfaction surveys (sent to anyone who has bought your products and has agreed to receive e-mails from you)
- one-to-one permission-based e-mails (personalising an e-mail message by naming both sender and recipient, the latter having given permission to be sent these e-mails; an example is an e-newsletter or 'e-zine' [electronic magazine] to which the recipient has subscribed; see Boxes 8.6 and 8.7)

BOX 8.6 Marketing via e-newsletters

E-mailing a one-page newsletter about your business (e.g., new products, new services, special offers, success stories, customer feedback, stories likely to interest your recipients) is a great e-mail marketing tool. It's important to ensure that the e-newsletter is well designed, interesting and sent regularly (ideally, monthly). Make sure your contact information is prominent, use catchy headings, include a link to your website and give the recipient the option of forwarding the newsletter on to someone else.

BOX 8.7 Permission-based e-mail marketing

In many countries it's now illegal to send unsolicited e-mails (spam). Permission-based e-mail marketing (also called 'opt-in e-mail marketing') requires asking people if you can add them to your mailing list. When they say 'yes' by entering their e-mail address in a sign-up box, you can add them to the mailing lists for your e-mail marketing campaigns. It creates a good impression if, in these campaigns, you also give recipients the option to opt out (unsubscribe).

The easiest way to conduct an e-mail marketing campaign is to use recommended e-mail service providers (ESPs), who will give you the software to create your message, target it, send it out and track the results online (see Figure 8.5, colour page VII).

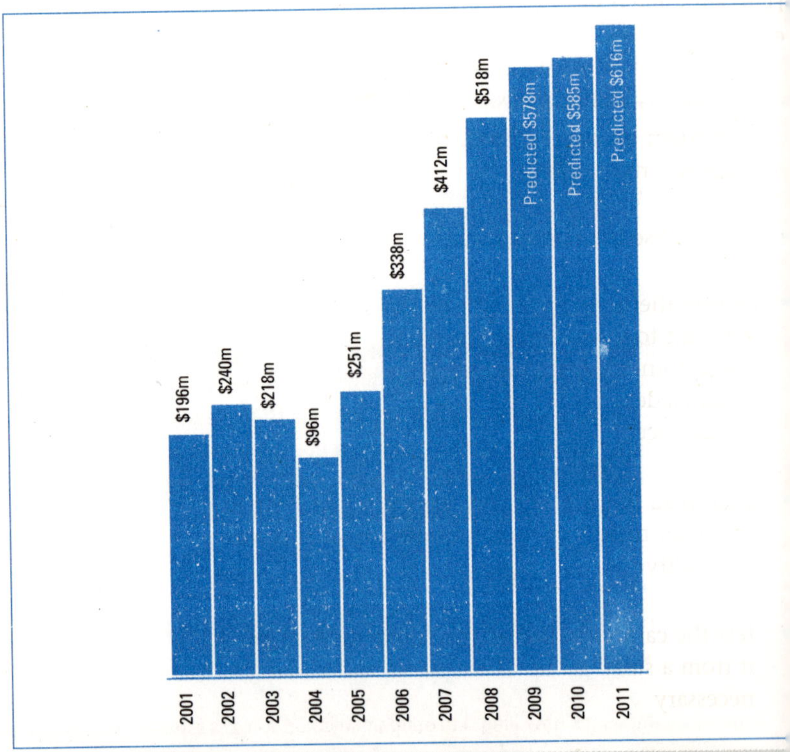

FIGURE 8.4 E-mail marketing expenditure, USA

The expenditure on e-mail marketing is likely to increase greatly worldwide in the next few years. In the USA, it is predicted to increase by 19% between 2008 and 2011.

Source: www.e-consultancy.com

Using ESPs will give your campaign a professional look and reduce the risk of your system freezing under the weight of the large bandwidth that is needed for mass mailings. It will also reduce the possibility of your domain being blacklisted by the search engines.

Here are some other tips that should help you implement successful e-mail marketing campaigns:

- aim the campaign at specific segments where possible, keeping the campaign message relevant to the recipient ('right person, right message, right time')
- personalise the message where possible
- ensure the heading (or title or subject line) is compelling and relevant to your message (some software packages will use many subject lines initially in sample e-mails to see which line compels most readers to open the e-mail, and then send out the rest of the e-mails accordingly)
- proofread the content very carefully – spelling mistakes and poor grammar make you look unprofessional and will erode campaign credibility
- test the campaign before you implement it, gauging the reaction to it from a small group of recipients and making any amendments necessary
- launch the campaign when you think you are most likely to get the best response rate (e.g., some marketers say that it's best to send B2B e-mails at 11 a.m. on a Wednesday and B2C e-mails at weekends or in the evenings when people are opening their personal inbox)

- keep your data (e.g., mailing lists, sending dates, recipient numbers) in good order so that you can accurately measure your campaign results
- use the data and experiences from past e-mail marketing campaigns to tailor new campaigns

With many large and medium-sized businesses now making e-mail marketing an essential part of their marketing mix, it's an approach that you can't afford to ignore. As with all e-marketing tools, it doesn't cost much, requires creativity, planning and organisation, is a great way to boost brand awareness and can be very rewarding.

Chapter 9

MANAGEMENT

YOU HAVE A NEW BUSINESS website. It looks good, functions well, is informative and interesting, has streamlined many of your business operations, sits high in the organic listings, is drawing in the crowds and is bringing in the revenue. Now what? Relax? Put your feet up? Go golfing?

No, your website work has really only just begun. Whatever the size of your site – small or corporate – it has to be managed, constantly and creatively. If this isn't done, the site will soon lose its vitality, begin to age and start looking a bit mouldy. And you will have wasted all the effort and expense it took to create it. In today's world, a business with a poorly managed website will very soon be a business without business.

Managing a website involves using a content management system (CMS). A CMS is what it says – software (off-the-shelf, modified or bespoke) for managing (editing, maintaining, supplementing, updating) the content (text, images, audio files, electronic documents, etc.) on your website. Unlike many applications for websites, a CMS caters for users who need not have great website skills or know anything about computer languages, and yet, using the system, will feel comfortable making changes to website content.

There are many approaches to content management and many CMS packages for sale or hire. You need to decide what suits you. Ask yourself: How much will I need to change on the website? This is the pivotal question when deciding on the best CMS for you.

Then ask yourself two important supplementary questions: What is my content management budget? What in-house resources do I have for content management? This chapter covers the factors you need to bear in mind when answering these questions, shows you the benefits of a CMS and describes what options you have when it comes to choosing a CMS that suits your business, your resources and your objectives.

BOX 9.1 Content management terms

'CMS' is used here to mean 'content management system'; you'll also see it described as 'content management software' which, in this context, is the same thing. Strictly speaking, WCM (web content management) is a CMS with additional management features, but we use the generic term CMS to cover WCM systems as well. Where a CMS is used for a corporate site or portal, it's called an 'enterprise content management system' (ECMS).

What do you need to manage?

You read earlier that there are three basic elements that make up a website – presentation, content and architecture. Managing the presentation and architecture is usually something best left to the experts, especially for small to medium-sized businesses, but this is not the case with content. Here, your web development agency creates the templates in which the content is placed (by you or the web developer) and then you, using a CMS that the web developer has created for your site or a CMS that you've bought or hired, manage that content.

The main content management tasks involve:

- editing content (e.g., checking accuracy, correcting errors, ensuring consistency, changing the focus)
- updating content (e.g., keeping information up to date, deleting anything that dates the site or is no longer relevant, such as past special offers)
- creating content (e.g., devising new product categories / pages, putting together community areas, writing blogs, press releases and newsletters)
- adding content (e.g., uploading PDF documents, podcasts and videos)

This involves working at both the front end (the website pages) and the back end (the databases) where all the site content is stored and accessed via a secure and simple administration area.

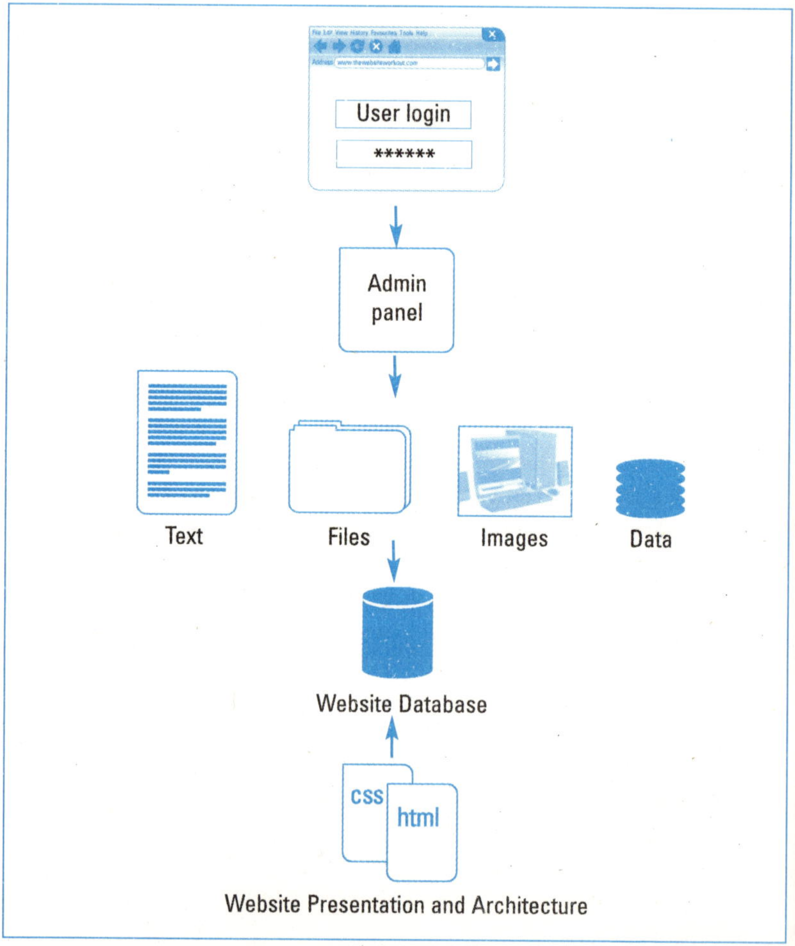

FIGURE 9.1 Amending content via a content management system (CMS)

A good CMS enables you to access the area of your site (see Figure 9.2) where you can easily add, remove, amend and update site text, files (e.g., PDFs), images and data.

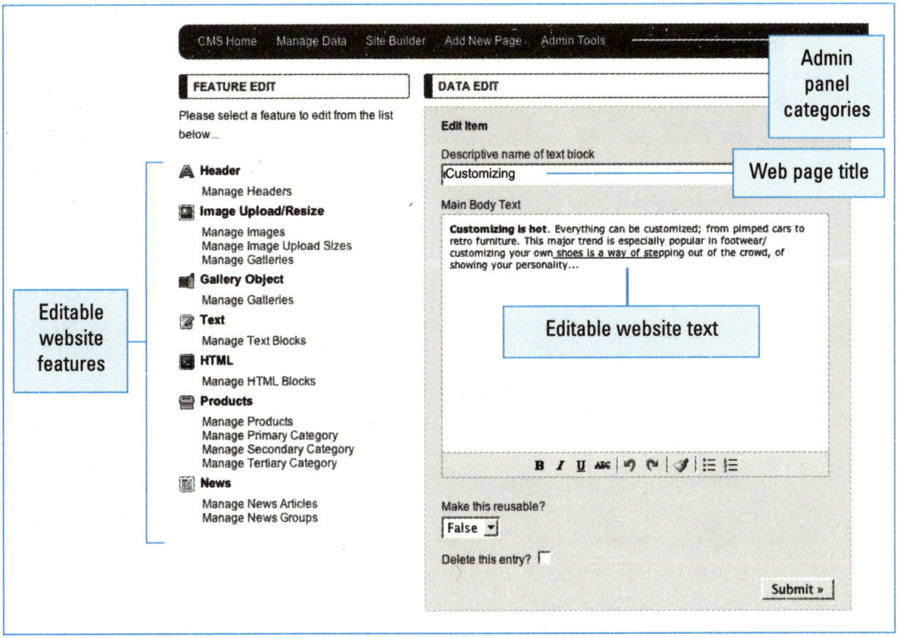

FIGURE 9.2 Content management area

A good content management area is simple and well categorised, with a facility for editing text using the usual text tools, making it easy to use for people who might not have much technical expertise.

What are the benefits of a CMS?

Business leaders around the world are realising that, in order to maintain a dynamic, revenue-generating website in today's globalised economy, they need to be able to manage their websites when they want, how they want and where they want – and this is what a good CMS delivers.

While the cost of investing in a good CMS can be considerable, the benefits are worth every penny. These benefits include:

- *professionalism:* a site with a good CMS will look clean, efficient, accurate and up to date, all vital attributes in persuading visitors to explore the site; sites that are clearly out of date, or never seem to change, will see visitor numbers dropping off

- *collaboration:* with a site that relies on authorised staff working in different places to manage it, a CMS enables them to make changes easily, see each other's changes, seek approval for changes, suggest further changes, and so on

- *content syndication:* a CMS can be used to pull relevant content automatically from other sites, as well as supply other sites with content from your site, according to set instructions

- *cost reduction:* with a CMS, many tasks traditionally performed by admin staff can be done automatically; there is less need for help from in-house IT staff or an external web development agency; better managed online customer services means less reliance on costly call centres; and spending on software is reduced

- *pre-emptive tasks:* a CMS allows you to specify dates on which new content should be added and old content removed, or when an updated version of something (e.g., a press release) should replace what's currently there, and will then alert you when it's time to carry out these tasks, or will carry out the tasks itself, letting you know when it has done so

- *speed of operation:* with a CMS, urgent changes can be made immediately, no need to wait till your web development agency has the time to do it; this is especially useful if the site is carrying incorrect information which, if not corrected quickly, could cost money, time and/or reputation (see Box 9.3)

BOX 9.2 CMS for extranets, intranets, microsites and portals

As well as managing a website, a CMS can also be used to manage intranets (a resource linking employees/members of an organisation/group), extranets (an extension of an intranet, giving authorised outsiders access to the site), microsites and portals (reached via the main site and usually focusing on one topic). It makes communication between people, departments, offices and countries, as well as between a business and its target customer groups, not only easier but more easily tracked and monitored.

A type of CMS that is becoming increasingly popular with businesses is a wiki; it facilitates the process of creating a document collaboratively. If you have staff scattered around the country or in different countries and need to get a major document together fast, and looking good, a wiki is a good way to go. An obvious example is the Wikipedia, which is based on a wiki that enables anyone, anywhere, to add to this online encyclopaedia.

BOX 9.3 Avoiding embarrassment

Without a good CMS, this could happen to you…

An online retailer in the USA received about 6,000 orders for a $544 monitor that had gone on sale online, by mistake, for $144. The retailer didn't have the in-house CMS capacity to replace the '$144' by '$544' quickly enough to prevent a lot of money being lost.

Getting their site's Terms & Conditions absolutely correct cost one company several weeks' delay in launching their site because, without the collaborative participation that a CMS offers, every time one person made a change the whole document had to go through the sign-off process again.

In a parting shot to a company, a dismissed web developer replaced the photos of the company's board members with photos of sheep. No one else knew how to operate the CMS. It took more than a week to put the right images back on the site. A serious loss of face…

The CMS market is relatively new and is expanding phenomenally. There is now a huge choice of systems and providers out there, ranging from free tools for individual site owners to expensive high-end ECMS solutions for large companies. The options available can be divided into:

- using an external agency to manage the site
- buying off-the-shelf software
- choosing a managed / hosted or licensed system
- going for a bespoke CMS

External management

There are many individual site owners who find it more cost-effective to ask a web development agency to spend a couple of hours a month on their site, making necessary changes and charging a fee for the work. They get this service built into their support contract.

The external management option could be right for you if:

- your site is small (less than about 30 pages) and the content doesn't need frequent updating
- you lack the time or resources to manage the site more cost-effectively than an external agency could
- your content is not integrated with other channels such as e-newsletters, retail outlets or warehouses
- you don't offer site visitors opportunities to contribute to the site via, say, a community area
- you don't need to update login areas

But should any of these factors change, you'll probably need to go for another option.

Off-the-shelf software

This is the option preferred by most owners of small sites. Gradually, these sites are being transformed into CSS-based sites, but there are still

BOX 9.4 CMS for table-based websites

If you want a CMS package but have a table-based site, you could do one of two things:

- Ask a web development agency to turn it into a CSS-based site. From all you've read in this book, you'll see by now that this is the way to go. It need not be expensive. And it would probably be cost-effective to ask the agency, while they're doing this, to add updates, upgrade some of the functions, do some SEO work and add a CMS.
- Alternatively, choose an off-the-shelf CMS for a table-based site. Among the best ones available currently are Adobe's Contribute package and WordPress. Note that both of these applications are also available for CSS-based sites.

many table-based sites out there. If yours is among them, Box 9.4 gives some guidance on what to do.

For CSS-based sites, the most popular system currently available is the latest edition of Contribute, called Contribute CS3. It can be bought alone or as part of the Adobe Creative Suite 3 package. Among the tasks it enables you to do are: control metadata, validate the code and update text, images, files and data.

The off-the-shelf option could be right for you if:

- your site is small and uncomplicated
- you don't have in-house IT staff, but do have some computer literacy
- you need to make changes to the content at least weekly

Managed / hosted and licensed systems

This involves CMS providers – companies that have created a CMS that you can use, for a fee.

With a managed / hosted solution, the CMS is hosted on the provider's server, but it's on your domain and you can use it to manage your site content, for a monthly fee. When choosing this route, you need to make sure that the CMS on offer has been created in CSS if your site is CSS-based.

With a licensed solution, you in effect rent the CMS from a provider and host it on your server. You're buying the right to use the application and will generally be charged a one-off or annual licence fee for this. You cannot sell it or pass it on to others; it's for your use only.

The managed / hosted or licensed option could be right for you if:

- you have a reasonable budget
- you need to change your site quite often
- you have the computer literacy and in-house resources to manage the site and handle hosting and scalability

BOX 9.5 Choosing off-the-shelf, hosted or licensed CMS packages

Here are some things to do when deciding whether to go for off-the-shelf, licensed or managed / hosted CMS packages:

- assess your current needs carefully
- think about your future needs
- assess your resources carefully
- assess the costs and impact on company resources
- assess the provider
- thoroughly evaluate and test the CMS package before buying it

Bespoke systems

With off-the-shelf, managed / hosted and licensed systems, you're constrained by the assumptions that those applications make about your business. They deal in generalities because they want to reach as wide an audience as possible.

With a bespoke system, there are no assumptions being made about your business. A web development agency will look at your business processes, needs and growth prospects in detail, and provide a CMS that fits.

Some agencies might build the system from scratch, but the more common route is for them to license a CMS, host it, modify it to suit your particular needs and then train you how to use it. They will charge you a monthly fee for licensing and hosting the system. They will often license the application for only one domain; if you use the same CMS for another domain, you have to pay a separate licence fee.

BOX 9.6 Going for a bespoke CMS

Businesses usually decide to go for a bespoke CMS when:

- they have a website, but need to update the content; the web development agency will ask what aspects of the CMS need changing and will build a small application to handle these tasks and integrate it into the overall CMS
- they want a new website and a bespoke CMS to manage it; the web development agency builds the site and then builds the CMS either from scratch or by modfying a suitable existing package

In both cases, before a CMS goes live, the web development agency should provide training in how to use it, as well as ongoing support.

The bespoke option could be right for you if:

- your business is medium to large
- you run an e-commerce site
- you want a website that has a lot of functionality and needs additional plug-ins
- your site will be managed collaboratively and constantly
- it is likely to be linked to an intranet, extranet, microsite and / or portals

BOX 9.7 Typical features of a good CMS

A good CMS should have:

- *Easy-to-use editing tools:* Most CMSs have standard editing tools, enabling non-technical people to edit site content easily. With CSS this is now even easier to do.

- *Scalable feature sets:* Most CMSs have plug-ins that can be easily installed to increase the functionality of a site. A plug-in is a module that can be added to a site, adding dynamic capability to an otherwise static site (e.g., a discussion forum, RSS newsfeed, events calendar).

- *Web standards upgrades:* A CMS should be set up to receive regular updates that include new scalable feature sets and keep the system up to current web standards.

- *Workflow management:* A 'workflow' (or task management) facility should be a core feature of a CMS. It is a facility that automates certain business processes, such as getting updates signed off before going live.

- *Document management:* A CMS should provide a facility that manages the life cycle of a document automatically, from its creation, through revisions, to publication, archiving and eventual destruction.

Thinking about the future

Among the tips in Box 9.5 is: 'Think about your future needs'. I can't emphasise enough how important this is. You have only to look back at the emergence and growth of website technologies over the past decade, and the massive change in the world's use and expectations of websites over that period, to see how quickly things have changed. If they have moved that fast in only a decade, how fast will they move in the next decade?

Above all, then, your CMS must be scalable and adaptable, so that it can accommodate the changes that might be needed, without you having to buy a new system at great expense. Here are some of the 'future' things you need to think about when deciding on which CMS option to choose:

- people are beginning to expect a choice in the form in which site content is delivered to them, other than what's on a site itself; newsfeeds, podcasts and vodcasts have all become popular delivery channels in recent years and, no doubt, there are more on the horizon

- there is also a growing demand for site content to be delivered via a variety of platforms, such as mobile phones, PDAs (e.g., Blackberry, PalmOS and SmartPhone) and reading devices (e.g., Amazon's Kindle); any CMS you choose should be able to cater for these platforms

- your business might be small now, but will the CMS you have still be suitable when the business grows and you have a bigger site and more functionality? (Websites do have a habit of getting bigger; a good aphorism to remember in this context is: "Inside every small website there is a big one struggling to get out." Is your CMS easily upgradable?)

- websites are becoming more and more content-rich; as they pack in more text, include more images and add more pages, controlling all this is going to become a major factor – is the CMS route you've chosen likely to be able to cope with this?

- building sites such as microsites and portals around the main business site is becoming popular among medium-sized and large businesses; will your CMS be able to handle the management of such satellites smoothly and efficiently, and without great expense?

There's a lot to think about and plan for when choosing a CMS that suits your business. The good news is that the advent of CSS has made planning simpler. CSS technology is going to be around for some time and one of its many benefits is that it makes the scalability and adaptability of a CMS far easier to achieve.

Chapter 10

ANALYTICS

A COLLEAGUE OF MINE – let's call him James – had a meeting with a company MD who wanted a new website and had shortlisted a few agencies to build it. He asked James to outline what we offered. James said all right, but first he'd need to know more about the company. What did it do? What was its turnover? Where was it going? How long had its current site been up? What did the company want from the new site? The MD alternated between being abrupt and looking bored. His answers weren't helpful. Then James asked:

"What does your site do?"
"What do you mean, 'do'?" came the reply.
"Its performance, the conversion rates, where does your site traffic come from, where do people go when they land on your site?"

The MD sat up. He had the online sales figures in front of him, but as far as he knew no one had analysed the facts behind the figures. "Tell me more," he said. And James told him all about 'web analytics' – the term for collecting, reporting and analysing data on the behaviour of site visitors. The 'bored and abrupt' MD has become a long-term client of ours.

In a recent survey in the UK, only 65% of the respondents (SME business owners with a business website) said they used web analytics data to make decisions about sales and marketing. That left 35% who didn't. And who may as well not have a website if they don't know what it's doing. Would a shop owner not take note of what sort of people came into the shop, which area they went to, how long they stayed, how quickly they found what they seemed to be looking for, whether they bought a special offer item as well, or left the shop empty-handed – and then use this information to effect changes that would increase sales?

The picture is different among the blue chip companies. Here, the survey showed that more than 90% of them make extensive use of web analytics data. The big online names, such as Amazon and play.com, employ hundreds of people just to analyse site visitor behaviour. Such organisations see web analytics as a vital tool for making decisions about website content and e-marketing strategies.

This chapter looks at:

- what you need to know about your site's performance
- what tools there are to provide the necessary data
- applying analytics results to your site

Working with web analytics needs persistence and patience. Don't expect to master it overnight. It can take a year or more to learn how to collect and use analytics data to best effect.

BOX 10.1 What does your website do?

What do you know about the performance of your current website? Understanding the importance of analysing the activities on your website and making the necessary changes is pivotal to operating a winning website.

How do visitors find your site?
Where do your site visitors come from?
What pages are the most popular?
How many visitors are new visitors?
How many of them are repeat visitors?
What is the average time they spend on your site?
How do they navigate your site?
What is the conversion rate (from visitor to buyer)?
What is the 'shopping basket abandonment' rate?

These are just some of the things you need to know about your site if it is to achieve its maximum potential.

What you need to know

In the early 1990s, analysing site performance consisted mainly of counting 'hits' – the number of times people visited a site. But this became less useful as sites grew in size and complexity, and site owners began to talk instead about 'page views' (the number of times a particular web page was requested) and 'visits' or 'sessions' (the length of time a visitor stayed on a page).

By the late 1990s this was being replaced by the forerunners of the sophisticated analytics tools that are available today, giving you the site visitor behaviour data you need in today's market if you are to achieve and retain a competitive advantage.

These data include:

- how many visitors the site attracts
- how they found your site
- what search engine they used
- what keywords they used
- what part of the country / world they are from
- what page they landed on
- how many pages they visited
- what navigation method they used
- which pages are the most popular
- what area of a page attracts most attention
- which pages led them straight to a purchase
- how long they stayed on the site
- how many of them were new visitors
- how many of them were repeat visitors

In addition to these data, which should be collected on an ongoing basis, you also need to know the data from specific e-marketing campaigns (see Figure 10.1, colour page VIII).

What analytics tools to use

There are two ways in which analytics tools collect website data. They can be used together:

- *logfile analysis:* your server creates logfiles that record all the activity on your site; analytics software loads them into a logfile analyser and produces reports (mostly as graphs and charts)
- *page tagging:* this involves placing code (usually JavaScript) on each web page you want monitored; when a visitor lands on that page, the analytics software gathers information about the visitor and produces reports

The main types of analytics tools currently available fall into two groups:

- Google Analytics (www.google.com/analytics)
- advanced analytics software

There is a third type of tool, a traditional one that you can devise and implement yourself at any time – the customer survey (see Chapter 2). It's as valid a data-producing tool as it ever was, made easier today by being able to do it online. Many companies now integrate the old and the new, mapping online survey data against web analytics data, to get the fullest picture possible to guide their sales and marketing decisions.

Google Analytics

The first thing to say about the Google Analytics package is that it is free (although you might need a web development agency to install it for you). The second thing is that it contains all the basic reporting and analysis tools you'll need. Whatever other web analytics software you use, it's best always to add Google Analytics to your site as well, not least because it's good to have a comparison. In addition to providing all the data listed on page 144, Google Analytics:

- is easy to use (especially recommended if you're new to marketing)
- helps you find out which keywords attract target customers and are the most profitable
- shows you what landing pages and content are the most popular and the most profitable
- tracks all e-marketing campaigns, regardless of search engine or referral source, and is integrated with AdWords, automatically providing you with ROI data on these campaigns
- is a hosted service that runs on the same servers that power Google, and is therefore scalable for any size of site, from small ones to large, high-traffic, corporate ones
- is safe, guaranteeing to protect the privacy of your corporate data, which is sensitive information that you don't want falling into inappropriate hands

When using Google Analytics, you might need technical help to set it up and to interpret the reports. In 2008 Google brought out Urchin 6 (www.google.com/urchin). This provides more in-depth analysis and full support but, unlike Google Analytics, it's not free. Paying for this support, though, might be money well spent.

Advanced analytics software

Advanced analytics applications do whatever Google Analytics does, and quite a lot more. For example, a Google Analytics report will tell you that 5% of your traffic is coming from Germany, whereas a more in-depth report will tell you that 5% is coming from Germany, and of

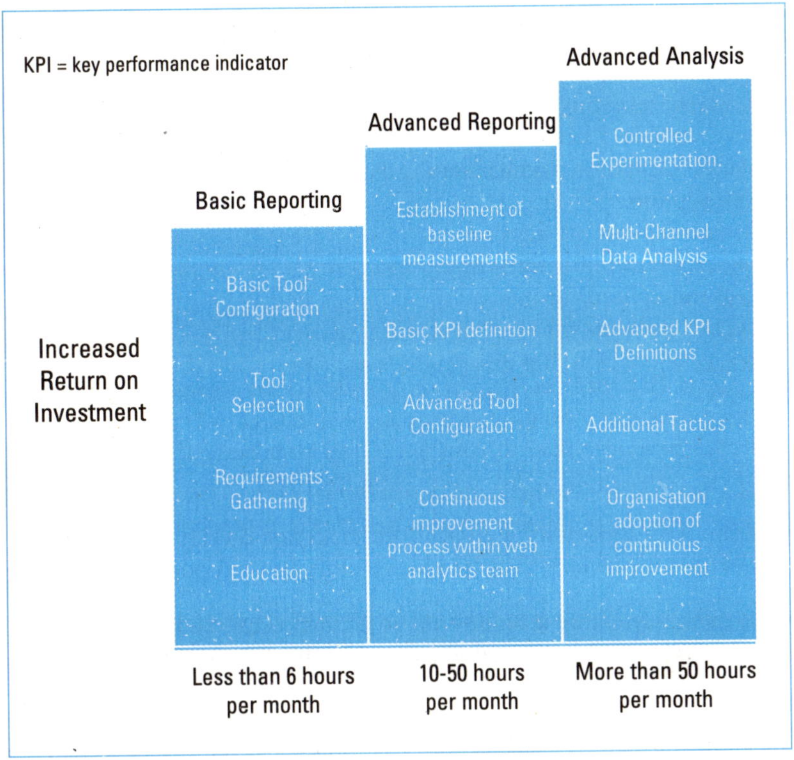

FIGURE 10.2 Features of basic and advanced analytics software

The first web analytics software began appearing on the market in the USA in 1995–96 and included NetGenesis, Accrue, Omniture and WebSideStory.

Today, the most widely used analytics packages are Google Analytics for the basics (providing the level of detail most small to medium-sized businesses need) and, for more advanced analysis, Clicktracks Analytics, Lynchpin, Nielsen/NetRatings, Nedstat, Redeye, Speedtrap, WebSideStory and WebTrends.

Source: Adapted from www.e-consultancy.com

that percentage, 33% is from Berlin, 20% is from Hamburg, 14% is from Munich, and so on. Other advantages of advanced applications include:

- bespoke reporting
- custom links / landing pages creation
- e-mail campaign management
- full support
- mouse movement tracking
- non-human traffic tracking
- real-time reporting
- reports automation

The Figure 10.2 caption lists the most widely used advanced analytics software packages. Should you use one of them? Or will Google Analytics be more suited to your needs and your budget? Here are some things to think about when making this decision:

- From your tour of www.google.com/analytics, do the reports and analyses it provides look detailed enough for your purposes?

- Do you have more than one site (e.g., microsites) and, if so, do you want to be able to aggregate data across the different sites?

- Do you have particular requirements about how you want content and / or pages grouped in the reports and analyses?

- Do you want in-depth analyses of the efficiency and effectiveness of the key processes on your site?

- How detailed do want campaign tracking reports to be?

- Do you need to break down the same data in different ways?

- Is geographic profiling of site visitors important and, if so, how much detail do you need?

- Will you need to run customised reports and analyses?

Licensing and hosting software

You can choose whether to license analytics software from a provider, or use a hosted service where you pay for the service rather than the licence (see Box 10.2). If you opt for hosting, it's common for this to be part of an analytics consultancy package.

The providers of licensed and hosted analytics packages vary greatly in terms of what they charge, depending on the technology, advice and

BOX 10.2 Web analytics costs

The cost of web analytics software should account for only a small percentage of your overall marketing budget. This cost can be difficult to assess when the work is spread between IT and marketing departments.

Licensing costs

- Providers usually charge a monthly or annual fee, or allow you to buy the software on a one-off basis for perpetual use
- The fee depends mainly on the technology required and the amount of traffic in the licence period; it might also be based on number of users in your company, and number of domains or servers
- You will also need to pay set-up and implementation costs (sometimes part of the licence fee), as well as maintenance costs (usually about 20% of the licence fee)
- There may also be costs for new versions and upgrades, and for business analysis

Hosting costs

- These costs vary according to volume of traffic and the complexity and levels of service that you require
- Charging is usually monthly

Other costs

- You need to factor in the cost of training and consultancy
- You also need to take account of the impact that running analytics software will have on the company's internal resources, such as the demands on the IT department

support needed. Often, the charge will also depend on whether you're operating at the SME or enterprise level.

Applying analytics results

Once you have the analytics reports, use them. If visitor traffic reveals, for example, that there's a market segment out there you didn't know you had, or suggests that the products on a page need to be re-positioned (see Figure 10.3), or shows a poor conversion rate or that most of your visitors are new rather than repeat visitors, you need to take action.

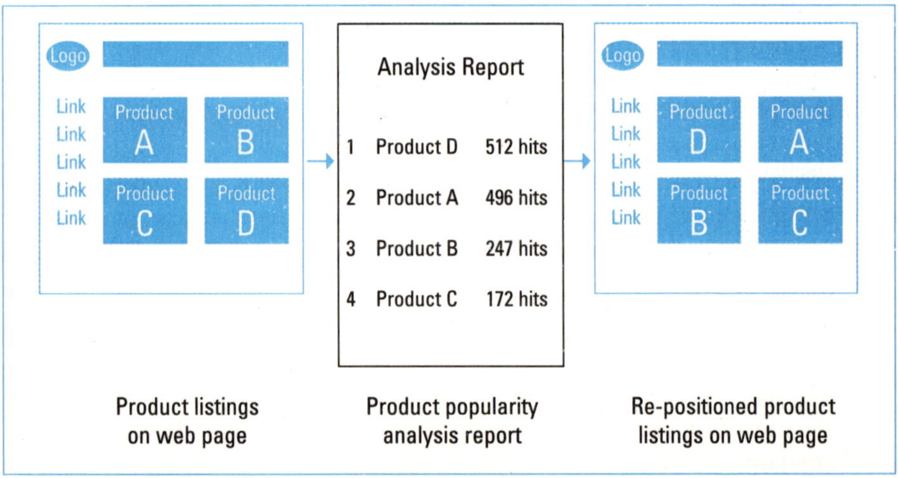

FIGURE 10.3 Applying analyses reports

This example shows products on a page that have been re-positioned in response to a product popularity report. As noted in Chapter 3, the web page area that users focus on most is the top left quadrant, so it makes sense to place the most popular products there.

I began this chapter with a story. So I'll end it – and this book – with another one. It is the story of a client mentioned earlier (Box 2.1) whose focus on analytics has brought great dividends.

The company began in 2005 as an idea – personalised 'talking cards' that could be selected, recorded and sent online. We thought the idea had promise and encouraged our client to research the competition before going any further.

There didn't seem to be any online competition, so the competitor analysis was based on looking at offline competitors, including major high street card shop chains and companies providing the machines in card shops that provide personalised talking greeting cards. Our client also conducted an online survey among friends and family and we sent a questionnaire to about 4000 e-mail addresses on our list to ascertain target groups and product cost and delivery expectations. We also looked at possible affiliate software, such as 'postaffiliatepro', and at recommended affiliate aggregate groups such as 'clickpro.com' and 'doubleclick.com' that provided reasonable commissions and were suited to novelty gift selling.

The research results gave us enough information to start building the site. We developed a bespoke e-commerce application and applied standard presentation principles with regard to layout, typeface, colour and imagery, with an unobtrusive two-colour theme, examples of brightly coloured cards on a white background, cartoon animation to give the site a light-hearted look, and clear guidelines in a clear typeface (Verdana) on how to select a card, record a greeting and send the card online.

Within the e-commerce package we built options for online and telephone ordering, clearly displayed, so as to reduce shopping basket abandonment and be able to provide information by phone because the product concept was new and might baffle some site visitors. The research had shown that most people surveyed had been very positive about the idea, but some were confused about how it would work.

We decided to use a fluid design to give the site more space for product advertising and to enable site content to be read on other platforms, such as PDAs and mobile phones. The research had shown that online sales via these platforms was increasing, and that many of the target group were likely to have access to such platforms.

We helped our client select the most suitable payment gateway and internet merchant account provider – one that would cater for a high volume of sales (about 1000 transactions per month) of low-value products.

The product information text was written up, with the keywords incorporated. The site architecture was built based on the prioritised web pages and a simple navigation system, and work was done on site branding and site content optimisation. A CMS package was built into the e-commerce package. Scalability was a major priority here because although the site would start with only about 50 products and a few categories, we reckoned that the number of products and categories would grow rapidly in a short time.

On completion, we submitted the site to the major search engines and directories, including dmoz and Google Products. As soon as the site went live we launched a Google AdWords campaign integrated with specific landing pages, as well as an e-mail marketing campaign aimed at reaching 10,000 people, including all those in the original surveys. An affiliate marketing plan, linking the site to complementary websites (e.g., stationery and novelty gift sites), was put in place. We also helped our client arrange some offline marketing activities, including radio air-time and magazine and newspaper coverage and advertising.

For the first 6 months after the launch, we met our clients regularly to examine the analytics results, and to apply what we learned from them.

The analyses showed which products were most popular, so we re-organised the navigation system accordingly and placed more images representing the product categories on the home page. It also became clear that the site was attracting large companies looking for sets of cards and good discounts, so we made amendments to meet this demand.

We analysed the AdWords and e-mail campaigns to assess the ROI and devise more campaigns. The analyses showed that we needed more specific landing pages for specific keywords (such as 'greeting', 'birthday', 'wedding' and 'exams'), as well as e-marketing campaigns that picked up on these groupings. After this had been done, the conversion rate doubled from 2.1% to 4.3%, a very respectable figure. The shopping basket abandonment rate seemed a little high at first, so we tried reducing the number of steps needed to order a card. This reduced abandonment by more than 10%. Within a few months of the launch, the number of visitors / click-throughs had increased by 300%.

Now, some 3 years later, the company directors have become firm believers in analytics, spending great chunks of time on analysing site performance using two sets of analytics for comparative purposes (Google and CN Stats). And their attention to analytics has clearly paid off. The number of products for sale on the site exceeds 1000, and there has been a very healthy growth in sales from 25% in year 2 to 200% in year 3. The directors estimate that in year 4 this figure will reach 420%.

It will, I'm sure of that, not least because they followed our simple but proven procedures from the outset and have put analytics at the core of their online business.

And if you do the same, who knows...

APPENDICES

Acronyms and abbreviations

API	Application programming interface
ASCII	American Standard Code for Information Interchange
ASP	Active Server Page
B2B	Business-to-business
B2C	Business-to-consumer
CMS	Content management system
CPC	Cost per click
CPL	Cost per lead
CPL	Cost per sale
CPM	Cost per thousand impressions
CRM	Customer relationship management
CSS	Cascading Style Sheets
CTR	Click-through rate
DDA	Disability Discrimination Act 2004
dpi	Dots per square inch
DRM	Digital rights management
ECMS	Enterprise content management system
EFT	Electronic funds transfer
ESP	E-mail service provider
FTP	File transfer protocol
GIF	Graphic Interchange Format
HTML	Hyper-text Mark-up Language
HTTP	Hyper-text Transfer Protocol
IMA	Internet merchant account
ISP	Internet service provider
IT	Information technology
JPEG	Joint Photographic Experts Group
JSP	Java Server Page
KEI	Keyword effectiveness index
KPI	Key performance indicator
PC	Personal computer
PDA	Personal digital assistant
PDF	Portable Document Format

PHP	Hyper-text Preprocessor (PHP)
PNG	Portable Network Graphics
PPC	Pay-per-click
ROI	Return on investment
RSS	Really Simple Syndication
SEM	Search-engine-based marketing
SEO	Search engine optimisation
SERPS	Search engine results pages
SME	Small to medium enterprise
SQL	Structured Query Language
TIFF	Tag Image File Format
URL	Uniform resource locator
VGC	Visitor-generated content
W3C	World Wide Web Consortium
XHMTL	eXtensible HTML
XML	eXtensible Mark-up Language

Glossary of terms

Accessibility: Making sites accessible to as many people as possible, whether or not they are disabled and whatever device they're using (PCs, PDAs, mobile phones, etc.)

Active Server Page (ASP): An HTML page that includes scripts that are processed on a web server before the page is sent to the user

AdSense: A method of website advertisements distribution devised by Google

AdWords: Google's pay-per-click advertising system

Affiliate marketing: Revenue sharing between website owners

Aggregate: Bringing together various groups of affiliates

Algorithm: Mathematical rules used by a search engine to rank websites in its index in response to a particular query

Alt attribute: A word or line of text used to describe an image (also known as 'alt tag' and 'alt text'; altermatie tecxt'; in some countries, the use of alt attributes is a legal requirement

American Standard Code for Information Interchange (ASCII): A worldwide standard for the code numbers computers use to represent letters, numbers, punctuation, etc.

Analytics: Tools to analyse website performance to assess return on investment and how to increase it

Application programming interface (API): An API enables different programs to 'talk' to each other. Developing programs which interface with the API can help site owners gain competitive advantage through performing more sophisticated analysis

Architecture: In the context of websites, the structure determing the organisation and labelling of information on a site

Autoresponder: Automated e-mail reply system responding to incoming e-mail (also known as a 'mailbot')

B2B: Business-to-business

B2C: Business-to-consumer

Back end: Those elements of a website that support the front-end interactions with site visitors (e.g., the e-commerce area that deals with the fulfilment of online sales; also referred to as 'back office')

Banner: Clickable online advertisements, which lead to the advertiser's website

Blog: A personal journal on the web (from 'we*b log*')

Bounce rates: The proportion of visitors to a website who leave after visiting only one page, usually expressed as a percentage

Brand: A company image, encapsulating the values and products of a company, represented by its visual identity via, for example, a logo, typography and certain colours

Breadcrumb: A navigational aid, usually at the top of page, showing visitors where they are and have been on a site

Broken link: A link on a website that does not take visitors to where they were supposed to go, often leading to a dead end

Browser: An application that provides access to the internet, such as Internet Explorer and Firefox

Cascading Style Sheets (CSS): A computer language for building and managing site presentation

Chat room: An area on the internet where people conduct real-time keyboard conversations

Click-through: The action of clicking on a link on a website, through to the next web page

Click-through rate (CTR): The number of clicks on a link or advertisement as a proportion of the pages or advertisements served, usually expressed as a percentage

Client-side: The components of a website that are visible to visitors, such as presentation (see also 'server-side')

Cloaking: Hiding an e-mail address (or other information) from spam spiders, using ASCII character code

Content: The text on a website; sometimes, it can also be taken to include the graphics on a site

Content management system (CMS): An application for managing the content of a website

Conversion rate: Relating to web analytics, the percentage of people visiting a site who make a purchase (converted from visitor to buyer)

Cookies: Information stored as small text files on your computer after visiting a website to accelerate subsequent visits to that website

Copyright: Legal protection covering the use and reproduction of original material

Cost per ...: Relating to advertising and affiliate links, how much an advertiser / affiliate pays per click; examples are cost per thousands impressions (CPM), cost per click (CPC), cost per lead (CPL) and cost per sale (CPS)

Crawler: Also called a 'spider' or 'bot' (short for 'robot'), the application that search engines use to crawl through websites and gather information about the web pages for their index

Cross-selling: Offering for sale products that are linked or related to the one a customer is buying

Customer relationship management (CRM): Managing the relationship between a business and its customers with the aim of building customer loyalty and retaining customers

Database: A collection of data stored electronically

Digital rights management (DRM): Relating to technologies that are used to control the use of digital media, and protect them from unauthorised access or use

Directory: A set of websites that have been reviewed and categorised according to sector, subject, region, etc.

Disability Discrimination Act 2004 (DDA): UK legislation obliging server providers to make websites accessible to disabled people

Domain name: The unique web address of a website, usually with the prefix 'www.' and a suffix such as '.com', '.co.uk'; there are no spaces in a domain name

Dots per square inch (dpi): The greater the dpi of an image, the sharper it is

Download: Transfer a file (often a PDF) from a website to the site visitor's computer

Enterprise content management system (ECMS): A high-end website management package, usually created especially for websites belonging to large enterprises

E-commerce: Online trading

Electronic funds transfer (EFT): Integral to e-commerce websites, the technology that facilitates the transfer of funds online

E-mail marketing: Online product promotion using e-mails

E-mail service provider (ESP): A business providing e-mail access, relating specifically to facilitating bulk e-mailing

E-marketing: Online product promotion through various channels, including e-newsletters, e-mails and banner advertising

E-newsletter: An electronic newsletter sent to a list of subscribers and containing news, information and/or promotional material

Extensible HTML (XHTML): A computer language and successor to HTML

Extensible Mark-up Language (XML): A computer language

Extranet: A private network that can be viewed as part of a company's intranet, but with viewing extended to some users outside the company

E-zine: Electronic magazine (similar to an e-newsletter)

File transfer protocol (FTP): Software allowing users to transfer files between computers connected to the internet

Flash: Adobe Flash, a graphics application that enables websites to use animation

Front end: Also called 'front office', those elements of a website that visitors interact with (e.g., text, images, navigation systems) and are supported by the back-end ('back-office') operations

Graphic Interchange Format (GIF): An image file

Graphics: A generic term covering the buttons, diagrams, drawings, graphs, icons, logos and menu bars on a website

Home page: The main web page on a site (also sometimes called the 'front page'), introducing visitors to the site

Host server: A server that hosts (holds) websites

Hyper-link: A link between one element in an electronic document (including a web page) and another

Hyper-text: The text on a website that serves as a link to another document (usually a web page) when it is clicked on

Hyper-text Mark-up Language (HTML): The computer language of the internet

Hyper-text Preprocessor (PHP): A server-side mark-up language

Hyper-text Transfer Protocol (HTTP): The protocol for moving hyper-text files across the net, which is why the full URL of a site starts with 'http'

Icon: A small image that, when clicked on, performs some task, such as linking (iconic link) or printing

Impression: The downloading of a specific file from a website

Index: The catalogue of web page data that is created by search engine software and viewed by search engines in response to queries

Information architecture: The way a website's content is constructed and presented

Internet merchant account (IMA): A bank account set up to facilitate the transfer of funds from online purchases

Internet service provider (ISP): A company providing access to the internet

Intranet: A private computer network within a company for internal use only

Javascript: A computer programming language

Joint Photographic Experts Group (JPEG): An image file often used for compressing still images

Java Server Page (JSP): A server-side language

Justified text: Text that is aligned on both the left and the right

Key performance indicator (KPI): Relating to analytics, an assessment of a website's performance from a business point of view, based on such factors as product conversion rates, sales per visit, repeat order rate and profit per website visit

Keyword: A word or phrase that is fundamental to the information being provided; also known as a 'query term'

Keyword analysis: A structured approach to identifying the keywords to use to attract visitors to a site

Keyword effectiveness index (KEI): A calculation that places a value on a keyword, reached by dividing the number of searches for a keyword by the number of websites listed for that keyword

Landing page: The web page a visitor lands on when accessing a website in response, usually, to a particular promotion that wants visitors to bypass the home page and go straight to a product page

Logfile analysis: Also known as a 'web log', a software application that records all activity on a site and is the source of data for analytics

Login: An account name (or 'user name') used to gain access to a computer network

Meta: In the computer world, a prefix that means 'about'

Meta data: Data about data, describing how, when and by whom a set of data was collected and formatted

Meta tag: A tag that describes the web page on which it is located; meta tags can be divided into meta description tags and meta keyword tags

Microsite: A small website, often only a page, linked to a larger website (also called a 'portal')

Mouseover: When the screen pointer (cursor) of a mouse moving over an element (usually a word) triggers a change in that element (e.g., a change of colour), indicating the element is part of the navigation system

Navigation: The system created to enable a visitor to move around a website

Newsfeed: News content published and constantly updated by a website that delivers it to other websites

Open source: Code that is freely available, the owner having relinquished copyright

Optimisation: Building and managing a site in such a way that, when search words relevant to a particular site are entered, the site will appear at or near the top of the organic listings

Opt-in: Give consent to be added to a mailing list

Organic listings: The lists of websites on search engine results pages (SERPS) that are ranked purely according to site content, not because payment has been made to appear in the listings

Page tagging: Placing code (usually JavaScript) on each web page that is to be monitored

Page title: Selected keywords from a web page displayed at the top of the page

Payment gateway provider: A service used by online businesses to allow them to provide online purchase facilities

Pay-per-click (PPC): A method of paying for online advertising

Permission marketing: Marketing to people who have given their permission to be sent marketing information

Personal digital assistant (PDA): A handheld computer (e.g., Blackberry, PalmOS and SmartPhone)

Platform: The framework (hardware and software) on which applications run (e.g., Windows XP, Mac OS X)

Plug-in: Software that enables features and functions to be added to a website

Podcasting: Distribution of audio or video content, typically for listening to or watching on a mobile device

Portable Document Format (PDF): A file format (Adobe®) that allows files to be shared with people who have different software

Portable Network Graphics (PNG): An image file

Portal: A small website, often only a page, linked to a larger website (also called a 'microsite')

Presentation: The 'look' or appearance of a website

Ragged right: Text that is aligned on the left but not on the right

Really simple syndication (RSS): Automatic content sharing between websites, used for newsfeeds, blogs, etc.

Redirect: Redirecting the URLs on an old site being updated to new URLs, so that the latter can be indexed by the search engines

Resolution: The clarity or sharpness of the text and images on a screen, measured on pixels

Scrolling: The movement of page content horizontally or vertically

Search engine: An application that allows visitors to search for information or websites on the internet

Search-engine-based marketing (SEM): Online marketing using the search engines

Search engine optimisation (SEO): Providing website content (especially in the form of keywords and incoming links) that is most likely to result in a high search engine ranking for the site

Search engine results pages (SERPS): The lists of websites that appear in response to a search query

Semantics: Giving meaning to website content in such a way that it will be easily understood by search engines as well as site visitors

Server: A software package that provides a particular type of service to client-side software

Server-side: The components of a website that are visible only to people with authorised access, such as databases (see also 'client-side')

Shopping basket: Also known as shopping cart, a software application that handles the process of online purchasing and delivery

Site map: A plan of the pages that make up a website, an aid to website navigation

Spam: Unrequested e-mails from strangers

Streaming: A technique for transferring data so that it can be processed as a steady and continuous stream, so that the site visitor does not have to wait for the whole file to download before viewing or listening

Structured query language (SQL): A computer programming language used to send queries to databases

Tag: An instruction inserted into an online document to indicate how the document should be read

Tag Image File Format (TIFF): A high-resolution image file format not often used on the web because TIFFs are large files that download slowly

Testimonial: Positive written feedback from a satisfied customer (also called an 'endorsement')

Title tag: Selected keywords from a site displayed on search engine listings

Traffic: Relating to e-commerce websites, the body of visitors to the site over a specified period of time

Uniform Resource Locator (URL): The series of characters that identify a web page (i.e., the address of that page on the web, which needs to be entered into the browser exactly)

Usability: A site that current and potential online visitors will find easy to use

Visitor-generated content (VGC): Information (e.g., text, blogs, videos) uploaded onto a website by visitors to that site

Web 2.0: Second generation of web-based services, generally used to refer to such services as social networking websites and blogging

Webcast: A video or audio broadcast transmitted via the web

Webcopy: The text on websites

Webmaster: The person responsible for maintaining the technical aspects of a website

Website bounce: Relating to analytics, visitors who get no further than the page they land on or who stay on it for less than 5 seconds; too many visitors bouncing suggests that there is something wrong with the content of the landing page

World Wide Web consortium (W3C): An organisation set up with the aim of enabling the web to reach its full potential

Selected references and useful websites

REFERENCES

Anderson, C. 2007. *The Long Tail.* Random House Business Books, London, UK

Davis, H. 2006. *Google Advertising Tools.* O'Reilly Media, North Sebastopol, CA, USA

Caples, J. and Hahn, F.E. 1998. *Tested Advertising Methods.* Prentice Hall Business Classics. Prentice Hall, New York, NY, USA

Carter, B. 2007. *Digital Marketing for Dummies.* John Wiley & Sons, Chichester, UK

Charlesworth, A. 2007. *Key Concepts in E-Commerce.* Palgrave Macmillan, Basingstoke, UK

Godin, G. 1999. *Permission Marketing.* Simon & Schuster, New York, NY, USA

Ogilvy, D. 1995. *Ogilvy on Advertising.* Prion Books, London, UK

Martin, J. 2007. *The Meaning of the 21st Century.* Transworld, London, UK

Meyer, E.A. 2004. *CSS Pocket Reference.* (2nd edn) O'Reilly Media, North Sebastopol, CA, USA

Nielsen, J. and Loranger, H. 2006. *Prioritizing Web Usability.* New Riders, Berkeley, CA, USA

Robbins, J.N. 2006. *Web Design in a Nutshell.* O'Reilly Media, North Sebastopol, CA, USA

Taylor, D. 2005. *Growing Your Business with Google.* Alpha Books/Penguin Books, New York, NY, USA

Temple, N. 2007. *How to Get Clients to Come to You.* Words at Work, London, UK

Sayce, K. 2006. *What Not to Write.* Words at Work, London, UK

Zeldman, J. 2007. *Designing with Web Standards.* (2nd edn) New Riders, Berkeley, CA, USA

WEBSITES

Note: websites come and go, and it's possible that some of those in this list might not be there at the time you read this book.

accessibility	www.drc-gb.org; www.w3.org
Adobe Reader	www.adobe.com
affiliate marketing	www.affplanet.com; www.myaffiliateprogram.com
analytics	www.google.com/analytics; www.google.com/webmasters
blogging	www.blogger.com; www.feedblitz.com; www.feedburner.com; www.feeddigest.com; www.typepad.com; http://wordpress.com
branding	www.brandchannel.com
business networks	www.ecademy.com; www.linkedin.com
code check	http://validator.w3.org/
copyright	www.netmag.co.uk/zine/design-culture/ copyright-for-web-designers
copywriting	www.words-at-work.org.uk
definitions	www.webopedia.com
directories	www.applegate.co.uk; www.dmoz.com; www.lycos.co.uk; www.yell.co.uk; www.about.com
e-commerce	www.e-consultancy.com; www.actinic.com; www.paypal.co.uk; www.secpay.com; www.worldpay.com; www.protx.com; www.verisign.com; www.nochex.com; www.netbanx.com; www.thawte.com
e-mailing large files	www.mailbigfile.com

e-mail marketing	www.aweber.com; www.constantcontact.com; www.glocksoft.com; www.infacta.com; www.pure360.com; www.dotmailer.co.uk
encyclopaedia	www.wikipedia.org
intellectual property	www.intellectual-property.gov.uk
internet advertising	www.iabuk.net
language usage	www.words-at-work.org.uk
links	www.linkpopularity.com
marketing	www.cim.co.uk; www.mrs.org.uk; www.wilsonweb.com; www.dma.org.uk; www.adma.com.au; www.the-dma.org
networking	www.ecademy.com; www.facebook.com; www.linkedin.com
newfeeds	www.rss-specifications.com; www.rsssuite.com; www.webreference.com; http://publisher.yahoo.com/rss_guide
open source	www.opensource.org; www.sourceforge.net
pay-per-click	www.google.co.uk; http://searchmarketing.yahoo.com
podcasts	http://juicereceiver.sourceforge.net; www.podcastblaster.com; www.bbc.co.uk
photos	www.alamy.com; www.dreamstime.com; www.fotolia.co.uk; www.photobox.com
reference	www.alexa.com; www.businesslink.gov.uk; www.webopedia.com
shareware	www.download.com, www.microsoft.com; www.shareware.com; www.zdnet.com; www.asp-shareware.org

search engines	www.google.com; www.google.com/addurl; www.msn.com; www.yahoo.com; www.yell.co.uk; www.altavista.com; www.ask.com; www.clusty.com; www.gigablast.com
search engine optimisation	www.searchenginewatch.com; www.webposition.com; wwww.wordtracker.com
surveys	www.surveymonkey.com; www.checkboxsurvey.com; www.polldaddy.com; www.snapsurveys.com
tracking	www.crazyegg.com
technical information	www.slashdot.org
usability	www.w3.org
website development	www.bcl-numedia.com; www.words-at-work.org.uk
webstats	www.sitemeter.com; www.webtrends.com; www.speed-trap.com; www.clicktracks.com; www.coremetrics.com; www.redeye.com; www.nedstat.com; www.statistics.gov.uk; www.worldmeters.info; www.infoplease.com
World Wide Web	www.w3.org

INDEX

CP = colour page

accessibility 28, 42, 62, 68-71, 75, 80
Accrue 147
acronyms 53
Actinic 100, 101
administration area 102, 129, 131
advertising 36, 42, 48, 59, 77, 112, 114, 116, 120-122
AdWords 9, 17, 91, 146
affiliate marketing 10, 114-116, 152
Alexa 21
alt attribute 56, 68, 70, 80, 88, 90
Amazon 97, 114, 139, 143
analytics 12, 141-153
animation 41, 42, 90
Ansearch 93
AOL 78
API *see* application programming interface
Apple 97
application programming interface 103
architecture 10, 26, 48, 62-81, 86, 129, 152
Ask 84
ASP 30, 62, 73, 77
AT&T 81

B2B *see* business-to-business
B2C *see* business-to-consumer
bandwidth 81, 125
BBC 119
Berners-Lee, Tim 27
Best of the Web 93
Bezos, Jeff 114
Blackberry 33, 139
blogs 10, 18, 48, 53, 59, 116
Bloomberg 119
bot 84
branding 3, 32, 34, 44, 72, 112
breadcrumb links 66, 67
broken links 92, 106
browser 27, 28, 30, 35, 38, 42, 68, 69, 73, 78, 88
BT 81
budget 12, 136
bulletin board *see* message board
Business.com 93
business-to-business 97-100, 125
business-to-consumer 97, 100-103, 125

capital letters 39
captions 36, 38, 39
Cascading Style Sheets 29, 70, 72-76, 81, 90, 119, 134, 135, 140, CP II
categories 4, 6, 32, 45, 52, 53, 64
chat rooms 21, 117
checkout 77, 97, 98, 109, 110
click here 57, 58, 68, 70
clickpro 151
click-through 17, 153, CP VII
Clicktracks Analytics 147
CMS *see* content management
CN Stats 153
CNET 97
CNLink 81
colour 26, 32, 36, 39-41, 58, 71, 74, 78-80, 151, CP II, CP III, CP IV
CommerceNow 100
community area 7, 21, 102, 129, 134
competitors 12, 13-24, 89, 91, 122, 151, CP I
consumer marketing 98
contact details 44, 72, 98, 108
content 10, 22, 23, 26, 47-60, 64, 71, 86, 90, 120, 129, 132

content management 12, 81, 127-140
Contribute 135
conversion 49, 142, 50
cookie 81, 115
copyright 31
copywriter 27, 47-60
cost per click/lead/sale/impressions 116
crawler 74, 84
Creative Suite 135
credit card 106, 109, CP V
CRM *see* customers
cross-selling 101
CSS *see* Cascading Style Sheets
customers 13-24, 99, 112, 132

databases 26, 30, 62, 73, 77, 84, 102, 129
delivery 11, 101, 104, 109
design/designer *see* web design
developer *see* web development agency
directories 5, 92-94, 120, 152
disability 70, 72
distributor 15, 19, 77, 98, 101
dmoz 93, 94
document management 48, 81, 138
domain name 3
doubleclick.com 151
downloads 26, 36, 41, 53
DreamWeaver 27, 29, 30

eBay 97
e-commerce 27, 34, 49, 52, 63, 95-110
EIN 119
e-InBusiness 100
EKM Systems 100
e-mail marketing 10, 112, 122-126, 148, CP VII
e-mail service provider 124, 125, CP VII
e-marketing 3, 12, 14, 15, 27, 85, 111-126, 144
e-newsletters 18, 21, 48, 53, 59, 77, 123, 134
Epages 100
e-shot 122
ESP *see* e-mail service provider
extranet 133, 138
e-zine 123

feedback 72, 102
Financial Times, The 119
Firefox 28, 30, 73, 74, 78
fixed sites 33, 34, 43, CP II
Flash 23, 41-43, CP II
fluid sites 33, 34, 43, 152, CP II
font *see* typeface
forms 29, 59, 60, 72, 77, 88
forums 12, 48, 54, 59, 117
Fox Interactive Media 97
Front Page 29, 30

GIF 41
Google 11, 17, 84, 91, 93, 97, 115, 120, 121, 118, 119, 145, 146, 148, 152, 153
grammar 50
graphics 29, 33, 41, 103, CP IV

headings 36, 38, 51, 53, 56, 71, 74, 80, 88, 90, 125
hidden text 90
hierarchy 36, 53, 80, 86
hits 144
home page 20, 43, 102, 104, 153
hosting 12, 81, 149
HTML 27, 29, 42, 70, 73, 74, 75
Hybris 100

IBM 77
images 23, 26, 32, 33, 41-43, 74, 80, 90, 128, 130, 140, 151, 153, CP II
incoming links 10, 21, 22, 23, 48, 86, 91, 92, 117 *see also* links
indexed pages 23, 57, 92
industrial marketing 98

information architecture 61-81
Information Architecture Institute 63
Internet Explorer 27, 73, 74, 76, 78, 87, CP I
internet merchant account 103, 152, CP V
Internet Service Provider 81, 92
intranet 63, 133, 138
iPhone 33
ISP *see* Internet Service Provider

jargon 53, 63
Javascript 29
JoeAnt 93
JPEG 41
JSP 62, 77
justified text 44

KEI *see* keyword effectiveness index
Key performance indicator 147
Keyword effectiveness index 89
keywords 17, 20, 21, 26, 56-57, 87-90, 120, 122, 144, 146, 152, CP I
Kindle 139
KPI *see* key performance indicator

landing page 121, 144, 146, 153
Latin 58
Lavasuite 100
layout 26, 29, 32, 36, 37, 43, 62, 71, 74, 151, CP II
leading 38, CP IV
licensing 12, 101, 136, 149
links 36, 49, 54, 56, 57, 64, 66-68, 71, 74, 54, 66, 67, 71 *see also* incoming links
listings *see* search engine results pages
lists 52, 74
logfile analysis 145
login 19, 44, 55, 88, 134
logo 34, 41, 44, 45, 66
lorem ipsum 58
Lynchpin 147

Magicalia 100
Maginus 100
mailing list 102, 126
managed/hosted 101, 134, 136
management 127-140
marketing *see* e-marketing
message board (bulletin board) 30, 117
meta tag 56
microsite 133, 138, 140, 148
Microsoft 120
mobile phone 69, 139, 152
Moneyspyder 100
Morville, Peter 63
Mosaic 78
mouseover 29, 58, 66, 68
MS SQL 77
MSN 78, 84
MySQL 30, 62, 73

navigation 11, 36, 43, 44, 53, 54, 62, 64-68, 80, 143, 152, 153
Nedstat 147
NetGenesis 147
Netscape 27, 75
newsfeeds 10, 18, 21, 36, 48, 59, 118, 139
Nexus 27
Nielsen/NetRatings 147

objectives 1-12
Omniture 147
Opera 30, 74, 78
optimisation 10, 20, 21, 55, 75, 80, 81, 83-94, 113, 120, 135, 152
opt-in 123
order confirmation 77, 108, 110, 151

page size 33
page tagging 145
page title 81, 87, 88
page view 144
paid placement 120

PalmOS 139
paragraphs 44, 51, 74
payment gateway 97, 103, 104, 110, 152, CP V
pay-per-click 10, 113, 120-122
PDA *see* personal digital assistant
PDF 53, 129, 130
Perl 77
permission-based 123
personal digital assistant 33, 69, 152
photos 36, 41, 66, 68, CP IV
PHP 30, 62, 73, 77
Pipex 81
pixels 34, 78
play.com 143
plug-in 138
PNG 41
podcast 129, 139
portal 133, 138, 140
postaffiliatepro 151
PostgreSQL 77
PPC *see* pay-per-click
presentation 23, 25-46, 48, 62, 64, 71, 73, 129, CP IV
press releases 48, 59
printing 81
product page 20, 104, 118
proofreading 53, 125
punctuation 50
purchase form 108-110, CP VI
Python 77

ranking *see* search engine results pages
Redeye 147
redirect 80
registration 104, 109
research 13-24
resolution 34, 35, 41, 78, 79, 80
Rosenfeld, Lou 63
RSS feed 118
Ruby 77

Safari 28, 30, 74
sales proposition 97, 104, 106, 110
sans serif 38, 39
Satyam 81
scalability 136, 138, 139
scanning 37, 43, 49, 51, 52, 71
scrolling 34, 35
search engine marketing *see* e-marketing
search engine optimisation *see* optimisation
search engine results pages 20, 23, 72, 90, 91, 92, 94, 84, 121
search facility 54, 66, 67, 71
SEM *see* search engine marketing
semantic mark-up language 70
SEO *see* optimisation
Sequel 77
serif 38, 39
SERPS *see* search engine results pages
server 29, 73, 74, 77
Shopcreator 100
shopping basket 15, 45, 51, 77, 102, 104, 106, 107, 109, 143, 153, CP V, CP VI
site map 44, 66, 67, 71, 80, 119
SmartPhone 139
Snow Valley 100
social networks 18, 30
speed bumps 86
Speedtrap 147
spell-checker 50
spider 84
sponsored site see search engine results pages
SQL 30, 62, 73, 77
SQLite 77
Starting Point 93
Summit Media 100
survey 16, 17, 123, 145, 151, 152

table-based 29, 75, 90, 135, CP II
Time Warner Network 97

title tags 56, 88
traffic 56, 86, 146
Treo 33
Truiton 100
typeface 26, 29, 32, 33, 38-39, 62, 71, 74, 151 CP II, CP IV

unjustified text 44
URLs 48
usability 62, 68-72, 75, 81, CP II

validation 70
Venda 100
VFunk 93
videos 11, 36, 42
vodcast 139

W3C 27, 28, 30, 68, 69, 75, 78, 103, CP II
warehouse 7, 102, 134
WCM *see* web content management
Web CEO 21, 91
Web Consortium 27
web content management 129
web design 26, 31, 54, 59, 64, 103
web development agency 31, 58, 78, 86, 91, 101, 103, 104, 115, 127, 129, 132, 134, 137, 145
Web Position Gold 21, 91
Web Standards Project 28
web-based marketing *see* marketing
webmaster 26
WebSideStory 147
WebTrends 147
wiki 133
Wikipedia 97, 133
WordPress 135
Wordtracker 91
workflow 138
World Wide Web 27, 74
WSP *see* Web Standards Project
Wurman, Richard 63
WWW Virtual Library 93

XHTML 29, 73, 74, CP II
XML 73, 74

Yahoo! 78, 84, 91, 120
YouTube 42